An adopter's guide
Life Gave us the

I'm Suzy, an adoptive mum to two girls who tiptoed into our hearts and lives as babies, four years apart. When we started to think about adoption, I struggled to find the information I needed about what adoption is actually like.

There are endless options for books about behaviours, styles of parenting that adopted children respond well to and stories of adoption journeys, but not enough on what the assessment entails.

I decided to write my own guide, from an adopter's perspective, to give those thinking about adoption an idea of what to expect. I'll share our approach and bits of our journey. I hope you'll find this guide gives you an insight into what to expect and how to begin to prepare yourself for the process.

Copyright © 2020 Suzy Stanton
All rights reserved.

Contents

Glossary

Adoption assessment timeline

Who can adopt?

Who decides a child needs to be adopted?

Part 1 : **Before you start**
Grieving
Finances
Getting your property ready
Childcare experience
Research
Paperwork

Part 2 : **The assessment process**
What to expect
Be open and honest
Stage one – checks, medical, preparation training course
Decision to move to Stage two
Stage two – home study, support network, be realistic, fostering to adopt, report, approval Panel

Part 3 : **Matching**
How does matching work? Name, matching Panel, planning meeting

Part 4 : **Introductions and beyond**
Introductions
Adoption leave pay
Meeting family
Routines
Being realistic
Post adoption depression
To tell or not to tell

Statutory reviews
Is it because they're adopted?
Applying for the order
After the hearing
Keeping in touch with foster carers
Life story work
Siblings
Financial help with childcare
School
Post adoption support

Glossary

Adoption agency

The organisation that assesses people for adoption; matches approved adopters with children who are waiting; provides ongoing training and support for adopters; provides support for birth families.

Agencies in England are either part of a Local Authority (LA) or they are an independent Voluntary Adoption Agency (VAA). The main difference between the two is that LAs have children in their care, and VAAs do not.

Social worker

Adoption social worker is the person who will carry out the assessment of people who wish to be approved to adopt. Each child in the care of the local authority will have an allocated social worker. Their role is to ensure the child's needs are being met.

Adoption Panel

Every adoption agency has an Adoption Panel which is made up of volunteers with a background in adoption or working with children. Members are usually foster carers, adopters, adoptees, medical advisers or education experts.

The Panel has two main functions. The first is to decide whether prospective adopters should be approved at the end of the adoption assessment process. The second is to approve a match between approved adopters and a child or children.

Care proceedings

These are the proceedings a local authority must issue at court if they have concerns about the welfare of a child and believe it isn't safe for the child to live with its birth family. The court makes a decision after it has read and heard evidence as to whether the child is at risk of significant harm if it lives with its birth parents.

Independent reviewing officer

The independent reviewing officer (IRO) is appointed during the care proceedings to make sure that the care plan is legally compliant and is in the best interests of the child. They are qualified social workers and have a duty to scrutinise the care plan and make sure, when appropriate, that the views of the child are taken into account.

Ideally, the same IRO will have the case from care proceedings until the conclusion of the case, whether that's by way of a supervision or an adoption order.

Adoption assessment timeline

Registration
- Submit your Registration of Interest with your chosen Adoption Agency

Stage One
- Medical, criminal and employment checks. Preparation training course.
- Should take no longer than two months

Stage Two
- Home study
- Should take no longer than four months

Approval
- Adoption panel decides whether to approve you to adopt

Matching
- Approved adopters matched with a child / children
- Match has to be approved by the Adoption Panel

Placement
- Child / children placed with adopters after phased introductions
- Adoption order can be applied 10 weeks post placement

Who can adopt?

You don't need to be married, well off and live in a big house to adopt. Adoption agencies are looking for people who can provide a safe, loving and clean home environment. They're not looking for the perfect parent; they simply don't exist.

You can be single, in a same sex or heterosexual relationship, married, live together, long-distance relationship and I'm sure lots of other situations I haven't mentioned.

Having a criminal record doesn't rule you out, it will depend on the nature of the conviction and how long ago it was.

Health issues don't necessarily rule you out. Again, it depends on what they are and how well they're being managed.

You can be renting, or own your home, live in a flat or a house. It just needs to be safe and have enough bedrooms for the number of children you're hoping to adopt. Any debts you may have need to be manageable.

Age shouldn't be a factor but the older you are, the less likely it is you would be considered for a very young child. Having said that, I was 45 and my husband was 54 when our youngest was placed with us when she was six months old.

You can already have birth children. There usually needs to be at least a couple of years age gap between birth and adopted children, but this will vary depending on the agency.

Who decides a child needs to be adopted?

It's important to understand the basics about the process that leads to a child being removed from the care of their birth parents. Ultimately, it's the court that decides adoption is the right option for a child, not social services. A social worker will start the process and present evidence, but they don't make the final decision.

The reasons why children need to be adopted have changed dramatically over the last half century. It used to be the case that children born out of wedlock had to be adopted, their birth mum feeling like she had no other choice. In the UK now, the reasons often relate to extreme neglect, drug or alcohol misuse by a parent and domestic violence.

Children who need to be adopted are likely to have suffered some level of trauma in their early years. This can lead to a whole host of issues for them as they grow up such as behavioural and attachment issues as well as issues with their physical health.

The process that leads a child to be adopted is often a lengthy one. It starts with social services becoming involved with the family, sometimes voluntarily, sometimes not and sometimes many months before the child is born.

Ultimately, a child could be removed from the care of their parents if the concerns are that they are suffering, or are at risk of suffering significant harm. They will then be placed in foster care. Assessments of parenting capabilities will follow and if the concerns continue, court proceedings will be issued.

The aim is that those proceedings conclude within 26 weeks so that there is as little delay as possible in determining where the child(ren) will live for the remainder of their childhood. The court process will involve evidence from social services, parents, experts if necessary and the children's guardian being filed and then tested during the final hearing.

Assessment of any other family members will also be filed. It is then for the Judge or Magistrates to decide whether the evidence shows that the child will continue to suffer significant harm if they live with their birth parents for the remainder of their childhood.

If they do, a final care order is made along with a placement order which allows the local authority to place the child with adopters.

Part 1

Before you start

Grieving

People decide to create their family through adoption for a variety of reasons. It sounds obvious but you need to be clear about why you want to adopt before you start. It can never be second best or your back up plan. Adoption is a choice, but it isn't for you if you think it's a last resort.

Some have never tried to have a birth child so adoption is the first way they've tried to create their family. Many consider adoption after dealing with the brutal disappointment of infertility. Whatever steps you've taken to try and have a baby whether it's naturally, via surrogacy or fertility treatment, if it doesn't work, it's devastating. If that's the case for you, your heart and soul have to be committed to adoption before you start. If you're still hoping that you'll fall pregnant, you may not ready.

For a lot of women, their dream is to one day become a mum. The human race has been going for a lot of years and it has survived because women give birth. It's a natural assumption, therefore, that all woman can have babies. Finding out that you're one of the ones that can't is extremely hard.

I felt a total and utter failure as a woman when I didn't get pregnant month after month of trying. At the time, I worked in family courts managing care cases. It took every ounce of my strength not to shout and scream at the mothers in court who were not fighting with every fibre in their body to have the right to look after their child throughout their childhood.

How could it be right that they could fall pregnant at the drop of a hat but I couldn't? They weren't looking after their bodies by taking folic acid, or reducing their alcohol intake, or keeping fit. Or doing anything really that according to all the books I'd read, would give you the best chance of getting pregnant. Yet still they were getting pregnant, staying pregnant and giving birth. And in a lot of cases, a few months later they were getting pregnant again.

It was really, really tough sitting and listening to that. As hard as it was though, it started me thinking that perhaps having a birth child wasn't the way we were meant to start our family.

You need to give yourself time to grieve the fact that you can't have a birth child. It's something that your social worker will ask you about in a lot of detail, so you need to be prepared to open wounds you thought were healed. If you don't feel that you can, you probably need some more time.

If you've had treatment, most agencies want you to wait for at least six months before you approach them. That said, each person is different and deals with the grief differently and each agency is different as to how rigid they are about this timescale.

We'd been thinking about adoption for a long time and as I've said, I think I always knew it would be how we created our family. We did go for tests and the one appointment we had was enough for me to know that treatment (IVF in our case) just wasn't for us.

I'll never forget the look on my husband's face when the consultant did my internal exam. It felt like we were on a conveyer belt and that we would be the ones thrown off because we were too damaged to be worth keeping.

A lot of agencies would have wanted us to wait for six months after our appointment, but we were accepted onto Stage One, two months later. For us the testing was the end of the grieving process to enable us to move on to adoption. I wanted to know that there was a reason why I hadn't got pregnant as I knew I needed to draw a line under why it hadn't happened.

It's different for everyone but the most important thing is being open and honest with yourself and your partner if you have one, as to what stage you're at. You both need to be ready to commit 110% to adoption.

Dealing with infertility is brutal, particularly if you've been through miscarriage or grueling rounds of treatment that haven't worked. It leaves you empty so you need to be kind to yourself and give yourself time.

By choosing adoption, you're embarking on a journey which requires another level of acceptance. It's likely that your child will be past the baby stage, most likely a toddler or school age. You need to have let go of your dream of experiencing pregnancy and come to terms with not experiencing childbirth or nurturing a new born baby that grew inside you.

You'll know when you're ready to move on.

Finances

While you're giving yourself some time out from the rollercoaster of trying to become parents, it's a good time to get your finances in order. There are a lot of things about adoption that make you think "if I was having a birth child, I wouldn't need to do this". I thought that a lot and finance is one of those things.

The point is though, you aren't having a birth child. You're taking over the care of a child who can't live with their birth family and you need to be in the best possible shape to do it.

A lot of people who adopt have been through fertility treatment which is an expensive process and can leave you with little or no savings and debt. Not having much money or being in debt doesn't mean you can't be considered for adoption.

Parenting is expensive however you come to it so agencies are realistic about this but want to be sure that you can manage your finances. If you have debts, you need to be able to show that they are manageable and that you aren't struggling to make payments. If you are, you need to take some time to sort that out so that things are manageable.

We had our mortgage, car finance and a loan so we were by no means debt free. We just needed to show our social worker that what we had coming in more than covered what we needed and that we had plans in place as to how this would be covered when I was on the unpaid part of my adoption leave.

Most agencies want one parent to take as much time as possible off work once a child is placed, so you need to be able to show how you would fund that. I took just over 13 months which took every last penny of our savings, but it was worth it.

Find out what your employer's adoption policy is in terms of leave and pay. That will help you work out how much you'll need in the way of savings to be off work for the length of time you'd like. If saving isn't an option, think about what other options you could consider. Shared parental leave is worth looking into if you have a partner. If you are unemployed, you'll need to make enquiries as to what types of benefits you'll be entitled to.

Getting your finances in better order is a good way of feeling like you're taking back some control. You control how much you spend on certain things and getting the best deal for your mortgage / loan / credit card and other household expenses feels good.

Getting your property ready

Giving yourself some time out is a good time to look at your property and consider whether you need to make any changes to accommodate children. You don't need to own your home, but if you do rent, the tenancy will need to be up to date, whether that's a private rental of with a housing association.

You will need at least one extra bedroom and ideally two if you're hoping to adopt more than one child. If you live in a one bedroomed property, can you extend or is there a way of creating a second bedroom with the rooms you have? If not, you'll need to consider moving. The time to do that is before you start the assessment process.

Each agency is different about planned building work but most will start the assessment as long as building work is going to be completed before Panel. If you are planning to do work, speak to some agencies first to see if it is an issue as that may then influence which agency you choose.

Childcare experience

You need to have some experience of looking after children to be considered for adoption. If you're lucky enough to have children in your life, great. We have two nieces who we see most weeks. We had them for sleepovers from them being around three years old so we were able to show we had hands on childcare experience. Most of my friends had young kids and I was involved in helping out with a lot of them at some time or other.

Childcare experience doesn't have to come from being involved with your family or friend's children though. Not everyone has friends or family with children. If you don't and your job doesn't involve children, you need to look at getting some experience elsewhere. This could come from volunteering with children's groups such as Beavers or Brownies or at a nursery.

You'll need to be DBS checked. This is something which is carried out by the Disclosure and Barring Service (DBS) to see whether you have any previous convictions.

Whether you need to do this and pay for it yourself, or the group you're going to be working with will vary from organisation to organisation. You need to do DBS checks as part of the adoption process so you may as well get started with them beforehand to make sure there are no surprises lurking.

If you do have friends and family with kids, get involved with them a bit more. Offer to baby sit or take them out not just to show you have experience, but it also gives you a bit of practice!

If you've never changed a nappy and are looking to adopt a child who's still in nappies, try and find a way to get some experience. I will never forget how stressed I felt changing our daughter's dirty nappy for the first time. It was at her foster carer's house and even though I'd done it countless times before with my nieces, I was terrified.

Research

I can't stress enough how important research is. There are lots of books out there from reference books which provide facts, figures and theory, to books written by adopters about their adoption journey such as "No Matter What" by Sally Donovan or "And Then There Were Four" by Emma Sutton.

There are many blogs and social media accounts written by adoptive parents who are sharing their journey. They are well worth reading because they tend to give an honest account of the highs and lows of parenting an adopted child.

Instagram has an extremely supportive adoption community. Follow #ukadoptioncommunity and you'll be able to see posts from lots of UK adopter accounts.

I would also recommend reading about topics like attachment issues and therapeutic parenting. Attachment problems are common in adopted children so it will help to have an idea about it before you start. Having an understanding of things like fetal alcohol syndrome will also help, particularly when it comes to looking at your matching criteria.

Research the different agencies in your area and get a feel for ones you might want to look into. First4Adoption is a good starting point as they provide details of all the agencies in your area.

All local authorities are adoption agencies either on their own, or part of a regional agency. There are also voluntary agencies too. In general, a local authority will try and place their children with adopters approved by them.

Some voluntary agencies only deal with harder to place children, for example due to their age or their particular needs. Spend some time reading about the various agencies in your area to give you an idea as to who you would like to approach.

You can contact as many agencies as you like to get information from them and attend information evenings. Some people find that is the best way for them to decide who they want to go with. Everyone is different as to how they go about choosing an agency.

We didn't shop around. We approached the local authority for the area we live in and right from the first phone call, it felt right so we didn't look elsewhere.

One word of caution with this approach though – you will be limiting the children you can be matched with if you apply where you live because birth family needs to live a certain distance away. We missed out on a few links because of this.

Paperwork

You need quite a bit of paperwork in the early stages of the assessment, so it's a good idea to get everything sorted before you get going. We had a panic and had the house turned upside down because we needed a copy of my husband's decree absolute.

You'll need things like marriage certificate, decree absolute if either of you have been married before, a valid passport / driving licence or some other form of photo ID, birth certificates of any birth children.

Also spend some time thinking about who you'll ask to be your referees. You need three, one can be a close family member. We used my sister because of our experience with my nieces, and two of my close friends who had young children.

I did worry that it would be a problem that all the referees were from my side, but the reality is that no-one among my husband's family and friends have young children. It wasn't a problem at all and our social worker and Panel were very happy with the references we had.

Part 2

The Assessment Process

What to expect

Once you've identified some agencies you want to consider, make initial contact with them. When you find one you want to proceed with, you'll probably have a more detailed telephone interview and then a home visit is arranged. In the current climate due to Covid-19, an initial home visit may not take place and may be done via a video call. A lot will depend on the level of restrictions in your area when you apply.

The initial visit (whether that's in person or virtually) will be with one, possibly two social workers who will discuss the process in more detail. This discussion will be about the adoption assessment, how it works, what is required of you, time scales and the like, and also a discussion about your circumstances. If it's a virtual call, you may have to show them round your home so be prepared for knowing the best way to do that using Zoom or another video calling platform.

I was utterly terrified for our initial visit. I'd cleaned the house to within an inch of its life which included putting our empty wine bottles in next door's recycling bin just in case they looked in ours. Which of course they didn't. I even made cookies.

I think the social workers were with us for a couple of hours. One had a quick look round the house to check there were no obvious issues that needed to be put right. The only thing they identified was that a fence would be needed in our garden as it is quite steep.

You can still change your mind about going with an agency after this stage and you can have visits from more than one agency to help you decide who to go with. It's only when you complete the Registration of Interest form and return it to the agency of your choice, that you're formally saying you want to proceed with a particular agency.

Once the form is returned, they usually reply within five working days to tell you whether they are accepting your application. It was slightly longer for us first time round because the social workers who came out knew we were going to their information evening which was about 10 days later so they waited until then to tell us we had been accepted onto the next stage. It was the longest 10 days of my life!

One thing you have to be prepared for with adoption is the need to be patient. The wheels at social services can often turn very, very slowly.

Be Open and Honest

I can't emphasise enough how important it is to be open and honest with your social worker. Withholding information because you're worried about it having a negative impact on your application will come back and bite you.

There's no such thing as a perfect parent. We're all human so it's expected that there are things about you which aren't that way. Talk about them and put a positive spin on them if possible, to show what you've learned from the experience.

This is obviously a lot easier to do if you feel happy and relaxed with your social worker. We had a brilliant relationship with ours and found that talking to her about our lives, warts and all, was actually quite therapeutic. It made us realise that we've overcome a lot during our relationship and we'd come out of it all a much stronger team.

I would mention anything you're concerned about early on then it's out in the open and your mind is at ease about it. A common concern that people have is experiencing mental health issues such as depression or anxiety. I see a lot of questions about this on social media. Like all conditions and illnesses, as long as it is managed, it's unlikely to negatively impact on your application. It could actually strengthen it because it can show how you cope with difficult issues and get help when needed.

Depression is a common illness and is caused by a chemical imbalance in the brain. For a lot of people, ant-depressants are the only way of redressing that imbalance. Being on them long term doesn't mean you can't be a good parent. It's treatment for an illness just like taking long term medication for something like diabetes is. Talk to your social worker about it and show how you're coping with it.

Covid-19

It's probably a good time to mention the virus at this stage and the impact it will have on your assessment. Assessments are still taking place, but they're being done in a different way to how they happened pre-virus. Due to social distancing rules, rather than meetings and training being face to face, the majority are now done virtually.

You might find that you go through the whole of the assessment process without ever meeting your social worker face to face. That's sad. I know it can be difficult to get to know someone without meeting them in person. Unfortunately, that's the way things are currently and there isn't really a way around it. At least it means things can move forward.

If you're uneasy using technology or don't have a good Wifi signal, talk to your social worker about it straight away. It's likely that panel and meetings about family finding and matching will be video calls too. So, it's best to address any problems you have with it early on then they can be resolved.

You may also find that although there are two distinct stages to the assessment, new guidance has said that they can be combined. This means you can move on to Stage Two while you're waiting for things like DBS checks and medicals which may be delayed due to the impact of the virus.

Stage One

Checks

Once you're accepted, Stage One of the process starts which should take about two months. It's worth noting here that agencies have targets for how quickly an assessment should take. However, the reality is that delays do happen. Don't expect things to happen exactly within two months. Any delays should be explained to you and if they're not, don't be afraid to ask.

This stage involves your agency doing some checks and references with the police, the local authority, your employers (past and present where appropriate) and your landlord or mortgage company.

If you (or your partner if you have one) have been in a previous significant relationship, your social worker may want to speak to your ex-partner. Whether this is done will depend on things like the length of the relationship, how long ago it was and whether there were any children.

Our social worker didn't want to speak to my husband's ex-wife. They'd been together for quite a few years, but they didn't have any children so she decided it wasn't necessary to speak to her.

I know that this is something a lot of people worry about. Ex's are ex for a reason! If you have strong feelings that you don't want your ex being contacted, speak to your social worker about it.

During this stage, you'll be asked to provide details of your referees and complete a self-assessment questionnaire.

At some point during the process you'll have to have a DBS check. It's best to get these sent off as early as possible as it can be very unpredictable as to how long they take to come back.

The Approval Panel for our youngest had to be put back a month because our checks weren't back in time. I think they took 10 weeks. The checks can only be prioritised if you have a Panel date, otherwise they get done when they get done which can be very frustrating.

Pet assessment

If you have pets, some kind of assessment will need to be done to make sure they're safe around children. How and when this happens will depend on your agency. Some do it during Stage One, some during Stage Two. Some require a vets report which you have to pay for, some need you to complete a form yourselves. Ask at the start of the process how it's done with your agency so you know what's expected.

Medical

You'll need to have a medical with your GP as part of this stage. This is basically your GP going through a questionnaire with you, taking your height and weight and discussing any issues that appear on your records.

Some agencies pay the fee for the medical. If yours doesn't they should tell you about this at the start and give you an idea how much the fee is. If your agency does pay, it may take a bit of time to sort out the payment.

With our youngest we had weeks of chasing the surgery and our agency as the fee note sent from the GP got lost for both myself and my husband. The agency wouldn't pay without the piece of paper and the GP wouldn't let us book the appointment until the fee was paid.

As I've said before, if you're worried about something to do with your health, I would mention it at the start of the assessment process. Most people have aches and pains and often some condition or illness that they live with.

The purpose of the medical is to check there's nothing major going on that isn't being managed. If you have a condition or illness, how does it affect you on a daily basis? Will it affect you being able to safely parent?

Weight is an issue that often comes up. If you're overweight, are you doing anything to improve things? It's not about having the perfect BMI, it's about being healthy.

If you do have medical issues and see one GP in particular about them, I would ask to have your medical with them. They'll know more about you and how you're coping and managing the issue. That should mean they can explain it better on the form than a doctor who's meeting you for the first time to do the medical and is reading from your notes.

Preparation training course

At some point during your assessment you'll have to attend (either virtually or in person) a training and preparation course for three or four days with other prospective adopters. Some agencies do this course during stage One, some during stage Two, some do it split over the two stages.

There may also be some online training around the issues children who have been in care face and how to tackle them. You'll also need to complete a learning log of the books you've read and the training you've undertaken. Some agencies will give you some directed learning to do yourselves, recommending certain books or training material.

Be warned, the preparation course is emotionally draining. You'll receive a lot of information about a wide range of subjects. You'll learn about care proceedings and the types of things that lead to children being removed from the care of their parents. It's very difficult to hear about the circumstances some children have been living in.

The biggest part about the preparation course is joining in. It may be out of your comfort zone to get involved in discussions and talking in a group, but it's something you need to do to get as much as possible out of the course. Obviously, it's harder to be able to do that if the training is done via a video platform rather than in person.

The course isn't a formal assessment of you as potential adopters, but if you don't say a word throughout the course, or if you're very vocal and don't listen to what others have to say, that is something that will be taken into account when considering whether you should be accepted onto Stage Two.

If you're at all concerned about things, speak to the social workers beforehand. My husband was very nervous about having to talk in front of the group so I emailed one of the social workers (who actually turned out to be our social worker) before the course started.

She was able to put his mind at rest about what the course was going to entail and, in the end, he felt quite at ease within the group and he felt confident about joining in with discussions.

If your course is being done virtually and you're worried about using the technology, let your agency know. They'll need to put things in place so that you can access the training. Technology isn't something every can do easily so you shouldn't be at a disadvantage if it doesn't come easy to you.

I guess it's like all things that are different or new, you just don't know what to expect. Once you get there (in person or virtually) and meet everyone, you can relax a bit more.

There will be a number of different speakers who will give you information about various aspects of the process. We had a social worker, an adoptee, a couple who had adopted three children and a psychologist.

I was fascinated by what the adoptee had to say. It was really useful to hear about the process from his perspective. His birth mother was Irish and brought up in a staunchly catholic family. She got pregnant out of wedlock and was sent away from the family to give birth because of the shame it would cause if she'd stayed at home.

She was sent to a place in the North of England which was run by nuns for girls in a similar situation to her. A few days after she gave birth she was sent to the hairdressers and when she came back, her baby was gone. She was then packed off back home to resume her life as if nothing had happened.

It was the North East where she'd given birth and she moved back there when she was able to as she felt she was near to her son there. She'd gone on to marry and have more children but remained in the area in the hope one day she'd be able to meet her son.

The gentleman told us how he'd been adopted as a baby and had had a good life with his adoptive family and had always known he was adopted. His adopted parents had both died when he was in his 40s and it was only then that he decided to see if he could trace his birth family.

He'd been in a pub one evening with friends and one of them had pointed out another man in the pub and said that they looked very much like each other. He thought nothing of it but agreed they looked very similar.

After successfully tracing his birth family who were still living in the North East, he went to his birth mother's house. The first person he saw in the house when he was invited in, was the man from the pub who turned out to be his half-brother.

It was such an amazing story and very good to hear from adoptees point of view how he felt about having two families. He knew he was adopted from being very young so it wasn't anything different for him.

The couple who had adopted a sibling group of three were utterly inspiring. They were very open and honest about how difficult it had been after the children came home. The eldest was about seven at the time and had been taking on a parenting role to her two younger siblings while they had all been living with their birth family because of the circumstances in the home.

It was very difficult for her after she was placed with the couple, to let anyone else take on this role. The couple told us about the strategies they'd used to overcome this to enable their daughter be a little girl again. Two years on, there were still some issues, but they had all settled in really well and the eldest was doing better than anyone had imagined she would be.

The psychologist was fascinating and gave us a lot of useful information about a lot of mental health conditions. One of the discussions with her was about whether children who are adopted as young babies can be affected by issues such as domestic abuse which happened when birth mother was pregnant.

I was really shocked to find out that a baby in the womb can still be affected by not just physical domestic abuse but shouting and arguments too. The psychologist told us about a study that had been done to see if there if verbal domestic abuse had an impact on an unborn child.

I was fascinated to learn how they measured this. Basically they used a control group of pregnant ladies who played the East Enders theme tune quite loudly, regularly throughout their pregnancy.

The theme tune was played again to the babies after they were born, and they showed clear signs of recognising the tune. The study concluded from this that babies can be affected by the sound of arguments when they're in the womb.

The training also starts to get you to think about the types of things you would be able to cope with in terms of conditions and illnesses in children. I really struggled with this as it felt like by saying we didn't want to consider a child with certain issues, we were picking and choosing the type of child we wanted.

If we'd had a birth child who had an illness or genetic condition or whatever, we'd just have got on with it. It therefore seemed wrong to me that we had to say whether we'd consider a child with a lifelong illness or who was suffering from fetal alcohol syndrome or had experienced sexual abuse.

It's an obvious thing to say but it isn't your birth child. You're going to be looking after a child who has already suffered some kind of trauma, even if they've never lived with their birth family.

At the very least, they have lost their birth family and often will be removed from their primary carer when they move to live with you. That in itself is traumatic for a child, whatever their age. As is coming to terms with the loss of their birth family.

Saying that you can cope with a condition or issue when you know you can't, isn't helping anyone.

It is different if it had been a birth child. You may have found out about the condition when you were pregnant and so had time to come to terms with whatever it is and time to research and plan. If it was something that developed later on, you'll have been there for the diagnosis and so can learn to cope with whatever it is from the beginning, and learn with your child.

It's very different taking on a three-year-old child with behavioral difficulties or fetal alcohol syndrome. You have to go in with your eyes wide open and be able to hit the ground running.

Decision to move to Stage Two

At the end of Stage One, your agency will decide whether you can continue onto Stage Two. This decision shouldn't be a surprise. If there have been issues during Stage One, you should be aware of them.

If the agency decides you are unsuitable to go onto Stage Two, they have to give you a clear written explanation as to the reason why they have said no. Each agency has a complaints procedure which you will have been given details about at the start. If you don't agree with the decision, you'll need to refer to that as to what steps you can take.

If you're accepted on to Stage Two but something happens and you decide you need to take a break before starting, you can take up to six months. It might be that your agency has recommended that you take a break so that issues such as building work or employment can be sorted out.

Stage Two

Home study

Once you've successfully completed Stage One and are accepted onto Stage Two, you move onto the home study part of the assessment. This is where you have one to one sessions with your social worker (usually about six) where you discuss yourselves, your childhood, your relationship (if you're in one), finances, support network, the lot.

Honesty is the key during the sessions. It can be really difficult talking to a relative stranger about yourself and your most personal issues, but you have to so that all bases are covered in your report. Everyone has been through difficult times at some point in their life and this is your opportunity to show how you've learned from them.

You'll fix the appointments at the start of the Stage and your social worker will tell you which topics they're going to cover at which session. Our social worker gave us a written list of the areas she was going to cover and when, which meant we could talk about it ourselves first to jog our memories about dates and things like that.

I really enjoyed this stage as it was therapeutic talking about my childhood, my family and our relationship. It made me realise how lucky I've been to have had the childhood I did, and also how similar our childhoods were.

It also made me appreciate how much we've been through as a couple and come out of the other side stronger. I found that talking about our road to parenthood reaffirmed to me that we were doing the right thing for us in choosing adoption.

Nothing can be off limits here so prepare yourself to be opening wounds you thought had healed, particularly in relation to infertility if you've been affected by it. Your social worker needs to fully understand what has happened during difficult times in your life, how you got through it, who you turned to for help if you needed it, and the things you learned from it.

Families are complex and not everyone gets on all of the time so don't be afraid to say that if it's happened in your life.

If you already have a child, they'll need to be spoken to by your social worker. This will be done in an age appropriate way with you there, to see how they feel about becoming a big brother or sister.

We hadn't planned to tell eldest about youngest until we were certain it was going to happen because we didn't want her to be disappointed if things changed and it wasn't going to happen. However, our social worker needed to speak to her as part of the assessment (I don't know why it didn't occur to me that this would be the case!). I'm glad that she did because it meant eldest felt she was involved with things and it gave her time to get used to the idea of having a little sister.

The majority of the meetings are with both of you if you're in a relationship. There will also be one session with each of you individually, usually at the end. I was really nervous about my session. I'm not really sure why. I guess the point of the sessions are to check neither of you is feeling any pressure from the other about adoption and get a bit more of an insight into your partner.

Support Network

One of the key areas of discussion will be your support network. Just as not everyone has friends and family with children, not everyone has loved ones who live close by. That doesn't mean the end of the road for you if you don't have a physically close support network, or you don't have loads of friends and family who can help. Quality is definitely better than quantity here.

A support network doesn't have to be people who can physically be there with you. It can also be people at the end of the phone, virtual support or drop-in centre. I put down the adoption boards on www.fertilityfriends.co.uk as part of my support network. I came across the website when we were considering IVF as I wanted to hear about people of my age (at that stage late 30s) going through IVF and the levels of success or failure.

Reading the heartbreak that a lot of people go through during IVF treatments was yet another sign for me that it wasn't for us. I started reading the adoption forum when we were still at the thinking about it stage and I learned so much. I didn't post very much to start off with, but once we started the assessment, I posted quite a few questions and started a diary so I could keep track of our journey. I learned a lot reading about other people's journey.

Instagram has a great adoption community. If you follow the #ukadoptioncommunity, you'll find lots of brilliant accounts to follow. It's a lovely supportive network of people at various stages of their adoption journey and I would definitely recommend getting involved in it.

If you don't have physical support close by, think about who you would turn to in your hour of need. Do you get on well with neighbours who have kids? Even if they don't have kids, could you count on them if you needed help? Friends of friends? Are there local groups you can join? Are you involved in your place of worship? Think outside the box as to who you would get help from.

In reality, a lot of the help you need can be done over the phone. I can remember texting my mum and sister in the first few days of our eldest daughter being home, sending photos of a rash on her tummy to ask if I should be worried. Hubby took the same photo to the pharmacist and they all put our minds at rest that it was an end of virus rash so nothing to worry about.

Be Realistic

As I've mentioned already, one of the hardest parts of the process for me was thinking about the types of issues and conditions we felt we could deal with. This is something that is discussed in a lot of detail during your home study.

I felt much better about it once we'd discussed this with our social worker. She was very matter of fact about it. She said from the outset that we had to be honest about what we can cope with because we wouldn't be doing anyone any favours in taking a child with issues beyond our capabilities.

The person who would be most affected by this would of course be the child who will have already suffered trauma and upheaval. Being placed with people who can't cope with them but felt they had to say that they could, is not in their best interests at all.

I'd worked in the child protection arena for quite a few years and so was well aware of the types of issues children in the care system face. I felt that as young a child as possible was best for us so that we had the best possible chance of forming a strong and lasting attachment.

As much as I may have wanted to not have to, I knew I would have to go back to my job once my adoption leave was over. That meant being matched with a child with complex needs wasn't going to be appropriate because financially, we weren't in a position for either of us to be able to stay at home to provide the level of care that they needed.

The thing that I struggled with the most was fetal alcohol syndrome (FAS). I knew nothing about the condition initially and was utterly horrified when I learned of the lasting damage that can be caused by drinking alcohol during pregnancy. I knew it wasn't good for a baby, but I had no idea the extent a baby's development is damaged by it.

I really wanted to be able to say that we'd consider a child with the condition because I felt so bad that a mother could have caused so much damage to her child (perhaps without even realizing). The types of things that a child with FAS has to contend with varies massively, but it is usually behavioral and attachments difficulties.

We have two nieces who we see a lot of and we had to take them into account. It would have been very difficult for them if we were matched with a child who struggled with attachment.

You know what you can cope with and what you can't. Exploring issues with your social worker may make you realise you could cope with things you didn't thing you'd be able to and that you couldn't cope with things you thought you could.

It may still feel wrong that you're in effect picking and choosing the type of child you will be matched with, but it is a necessary part of the process to ensure that the placement has the best possible chance of success.

Fostering to adopt

Something else that you'll be asked to consider is at what stage in the process you'd like to be matched with a child.

Most children are placed for adoption once the court process has finished. This means that the court has concluded it isn't possible for a child to live with their birth family. Once the child is matched with adopters, final contact sessions take place with birth family and it is usually the case that they don't see their birth parents again throughout their childhood. Contact takes place by way of annual letters.

Another way matching can happen and a child placed with adopters is for them to be also approved as foster carers. This means when the child is ready to leave hospital following their birth, they are placed with adopters.

While the court process takes place, the adopters are acting as foster carers and so will have to take the child to arranged contact visits with birth parents (they don't supervise the visits, they transport the child to the designated place where a social worker will supervise the contact).

This type of placement has huge benefits for a child. It means that if the court concludes that there is no other option but for them to live outside their birth family throughout their childhood, they won't suffer any disruption in terms of their placement. Their adoptive parents will be the only carers they'll have known.

The downside for adopters is that you're the ones taking all of the risks. This type of plan will usually only be for cases where the conclusion of the court proceedings is almost inevitable. It's likely to be for cases where there have been numerous children taken into care and adopted and birth parent's circumstances haven't changed.

We were asked to consider it for our youngest but we said no. If it had just been us to consider, we might have been more open to it, but we had our eldest to think about. It would have been very difficult for her if her sister was placed with us, and then a few months later the court decided adoption wasn't the appropriate order and her sister was taken away from us.

That is what you have to consider with fostering to adopt. The risk of disruption and heartache are borne by the adopters. As adults we are more able to cope with that type of upset. But we're still human. I'm not sure I could have coped with that. Getting to know and love a child, particularly a newborn baby, and then for them be to taken away and placed back with birth family is very hard.

Only you know whether you are cut out for that. I guess you need to look at it more from a foster carer perspective until the court proceedings end. But I think that's really difficult.

A few months into waiting to be matched with our eldest, our social worker asked if we wanted to consider fostering to adopt. My initial reaction was yes. However, at around that time I dealt with a case at work which made me change my mind.

I was managing a case involving a young baby who had been placed in a fostering to adopt placement. On paper, adoption was going to be the conclusion because up until she gave birth, birth mum hadn't changed her lifestyle so that she could safely parent. However, she nearly died giving birth and had to have a hysterectomy.

Realising she wouldn't be able to give birth again triggered something in her. She did absolutely everything that was asked of her. She jumped through every hoop, did every assessment and course and turned her life around.

The local authority said at the final hearing that her efforts were too late, but the child's guardian and the court didn't feel that the evidence supported that view. In the end, the child went back to live with her birth mum after about a year of living in a foster to adopt placement.

I don't share this story to dissuade you from considering fostering to adopt; but it illustrates the worst-case scenario as a prospective adopter.

If you want to consider fostering to adopt, you have to do it with your eyes wide open. Talk to your social worker about it. Ask whether you'd be able to get in touch with others who have gone down that route in your area. Connect with adopters on social media who've fostered to adopt. Talking to them may give you the insight you need to make your decision.

Report

Once your home study is finished, your social worker will write everything up in a report which is called a Prospective Adopters Report (PAR). The report follows a standard format and you'll be given the opportunity to read through it and ask for things to be changed, if necessary, before it's submitted.

The only part you don't see are your references. If there were any issues as a result of what they contained, your social worker will have discussed these with you during the home study so try not to worry about what's in them. Chances are your referees will have told you what they said anyway!

At some point during your home study, you'll be given a date for Panel which your social worker is working towards. Having a date gives you something to focus on.

Once you're happy with the report, all you can do is sit back and wait for Panel date to arrive. In a lot of ways, it should be a formality.

Part of your social worker's role is to identify any issues as you go along and work through them, explaining fully what the issue is and how it was overcome or dealt with. They want you to be approved and will know if there are any weaknesses and address them fully.

There shouldn't be any surprises which is why it's so important to read through your report properly to make sure nothing has been left out. Don't be afraid to say if you think something needs to be explained in more detail or if you think it doesn't come across as you think it should.

Your social worker's manager will also have read the report and suggested areas that need to be discussed in more detail. They will have had regular meetings with your social worker about your progress so again, any issues should be flagged up by the manager well before the end of the assessment.

Approval Panel

As I said at the start, one thing you'll need to learn to do when you adopt is to be patient. The time from the end of your home study to Panel can feel like an eternity. I remember feeling completely out of control by it which I didn't like.

Up until that point of the assessment, we were involved. I couldn't get my head around how a Panel of people who had never met us, were going to be able to decide whether we were good enough to be parents, just by reading our report.

Surely the best person to judge that is your social worker? They've been through your life with a fine-toothed comb. They've been into your home (in person or virtually), met your nearest and dearest, and talked through your darkest moments with you.

That's where their report writing skill comes in. The Panel have to be able to see and feel what they've seen and felt, through the report. There is the opportunity for questions to clarify things, but the report is essentially what the decision is based on.

That thought utterly terrified me. Once again, we were bundling up our hopes and dreams and placing them in the hands of strangers and hoping they agree that what they read meant we could become parents.

There are three possible outcomes from Panel: you are approved, you are deferred, or your application is refused. The third option should happen very rarely. Any issues should have already been picked up. If you're deferred it is usually because an issue needs more detail or to be clarified.

There isn't anything really you can do to prepare for Panel. They are all run slightly differently so yours may run differently to how ours did. Adoption Panels are made up of various different members, all of whom have some experience of adoption or working with children in the care system.

I think there were about ten members sitting on the day of our Panel for our eldest. The chairman was a member of the council, there was an adopter, several social workers from different departments, a doctor, another medical practitioner, a foster carer, us and our social worker. I'm not sure I'd ever recognise any of them again because they were just a sea of faces.

We arrived about 30 minutes before our time slot and were greeted by our social worker. I think Panel was running slightly late. Our social worker was called in first and if felt like she was in there for hours. I imagined that our lives were being picked apart and every issue pulled to pieces.

By the time she came out to get us, I was beside myself and convinced we weren't going to be approved. I knew she'd said something to us, but I was so nervous I didn't hear what it was. We went into the room to be greeted by the sea of faces. Everyone introduced themselves, but as I say, I couldn't tell you now who they were.

I was completely terrified but the chairman put our minds at ease straight away and said the Panel were recommending that we were approved. The Panel then went on to ask us two or three questions about some of the things in our report. I thought this was a bit odd because they had already said we were going to be approved, and I was terrified they'd change their minds after hearing from us!

As I say, each Panel is run slightly differently so not all will follow this format. I sat on a Panel in a voluntary agency for about a year and they didn't do the hearings like that. We discussed the case first, agreed what questions we had and came to an informal decision. We then brought the applicants and their social worker in, asked the questions and then asked them to leave while we discussed the answers and then came to a final decision.

I was very overwhelmed by the time we came out of our panel. I couldn't believe that after everything we'd been through, we were going to be parents. It turns out that what our social worker had said to us just before we went in was that the Panel had no concerns and were very pleased with our application.

Virtual panels are done via a video platform. You'll be given instructions as to how to log in and what time. Depending on the platform, you may be put on a "waiting room" until panel are ready for you. The format will be the same as it would be if you were there, but you may have been given questions the day before so that gives you a bit more time to prepare. Once you've answered questions you'll be asked to leave the call and then your social worker will call you back when they're ready for you again and you'll be given the decision.

As I've said before, if you aren't comfortable with using technology, say so and ask for help. You don't want to be worrying about whether you can get the technology to work as well as the actual panel. Ask for a practice run so you can see how it will work.

Once Panel have approved your application, the decision then has to be ratified by the agency decision maker. This does seem to be just a formality and another box to tick. In theory, they could go against the Panel's recommendations, but I'm not aware that this happens other than in exceptional cases. They usually take about 10-14 days.

Part 3
Matching

How does matching work?

Matching is done differently depending on your agency. In some agencies, your social worker or family finder will do the looking. They'll look at all the children waiting to be matched within the age range you've been approved for, and see whether any are suitable.

They'll be looking at things like age, whether they have any medical issues and if so, whether they're things you would consider, background and location of birth family. If a child or sibling group seem to fit with what you're looking for, they'll make contact with their social worker. Meetings will take place with them and managers and you'll only be told about the link if everyone agrees you're a good match.

Some agencies do matching by putting the onus on you to you look at the detail of the children they have waiting and then it's more of a joint decision as to which ones you express an interest in. Some agencies also do competitive matching. That is basically where the child(ren)'s social worker meets a number of potential matches, interviews them and then picks who they feel is the best match.

Once a match or link is found and you've said you want to take it forward, meetings (either in person or virtually) will be set up with various professionals so that you can find out more information. You'll meet the child's social worker (if you haven't already) foster carer, the agency's medical adviser and any other professionals involved.

This is where you can get more information and the child is hopefully brought to life for you. You may get to see some video footage of them and more photographs which really helps to start to build a connection with them.

Once all the meetings have taken place and everyone agrees to take things forward, the match has to be approved by the agency's adoption Panel. This is the same Panel that considers approval, although it may not be made up of exactly the same people on the day you attend.

Some agencies do "bump in" meetings with the child before Panel which is meeting the child informally with their foster carer at somewhere like soft play. It may be that rather than a physical meeting, you can see the child during a video call with the foster carer. Whether and how this happens will depend on your agency and the age of the child.

Most adopters don't meet their child until introductions start. This is the process, usually a couple of weeks after matching Panel, where you and your child are gradually introduced to each other.

For a lot of adopters, the matching process is the most difficult part of the process. You're either picking yourself, or having someone else pick a child to be your son or daughter. You'll be making that decision based on reading a report and asking people who've met the child, questions about them. It's a huge leap of faith believing the match is going to be right for everyone.

Because of how difficult this part is, I've included quite a lot of detail here about our journey. I'll talk about the things we felt and experienced so that hopefully it will help you understand this part a bit more.

The way our agency did matching meant that we had no part in the looking at all. Our social worker would come out every three or four weeks to touch base and give us the tiniest snippet about children she had been looking at, but always with a reason at the end as to why they weren't suitable. That drove me up the wall. She only told us any detail and gave us the child's report when she believed it was the right match for us.

I was very naïve after approval Panel. It was September and I was convinced we'd be matched and child home by Christmas. Just typing that makes me laugh now. I was convinced our social worker was going to tell us she had a match the first time she visited after Panel.

She didn't and the reality was we were in for a very long wait. If I'd know that then, I think I would've coped better. For me, it was the uncertainty of the waiting in terms of time scales that was so hard.

As difficult as it was at the time, I think just our social worker looking was the best way for us. I'm not sure I would have had the strength to pick which child I felt was the best match after reading several reports. I'd have wanted to take them all home.

In the end, we waited 10 very long months to be matched. We tried to make the most of the time and did things we knew we wouldn't be able to do for a little while once we had a child placed with us. We went to the pictures a lot and out for tea. We even managed to sneak in a week in the sun to help take our minds off the wait.

There is no secret formula on how to cope with the waiting. Keep yourselves occupied, do spontaneous things and make the most of it are all good pieces of advice. Some people deal with it better than others.

I really, really struggled. I felt like I was in limbo and that our lives were on hold. We couldn't plan anything long term in case it happened, so were living from week to week.

I can remember having a dilemma because one of my best friends was getting married in the June after we were approved. She needed to know in January whether we would be going to the daytime, or just the evening. In the end I said we'd go to both as I was sure if I said that, it would mean we'd be matched before then. It didn't and we weren't.

By mid-July I'd started to think that it just wasn't going to happen for us. I thought we'd made a massive mistake adopting with the local authority where we lived because we'd missed out on several matches because birth family either lived too close to us or my mother-in-law.

I was losing hope. It became unbearable when we found out the final hearing for the child our social worker was hoping to link us with, had been postponed. A family member had come forward and wanted to be assessed as a carer for the child.

Putting off the final decision was absolutely the right decision for the child, but it broke my heart and really made me question whether I had the strength to carry on waiting.

It's funny though how things happen and I really do believe that they happen for a reason. About 10 days after we'd had the devastating news of the final hearing being put off, I got "the" email from our social worker that she wanted to come and talk to us about a possible match. I will never, ever forget that day and it makes me very emotional every time I think about it.

I was at work and for some reason, I hadn't checked my phone that much so when I did, and I saw the email, I couldn't breathe. My phone took forever to open the email. I knew the content of it was going to change our lives forever.

There was no real detail in it, other than our social worker wanted to come out and see us the next day with details of a child. I think I screamed when I read it. 24 hours seemed like such a long time to have to wait. I wanted to know everything that second.

I really don't know how I got through those 24 hours. Work dragged and I ended up being late leaving so I was slightly late getting home. Our social worker was already there with my husband and I actually thought I was going to burst. I was shaking. I couldn't believe that after all this time, we were going to find out about our child. Even typing this makes me cry.

We'd been approved for a child under the age of 24 months and we'd always said we wanted as young as possible. However, the longer we waited, the more I thought we would be matched with a child at the top of that age bracket. I was also convinced it was going to be a boy.

I thought I'd misheard when our social worker said it was a girl born just six months earlier. I knew instantly that she was our daughter.

We'd actually been given a tiny snippet of information about her three months earlier. There were a lot of concerns about her development when she was born and her head looked big and mis-shaped. I remember our social worker talking about her head size and that a lot of tests had to be carried out before they would consider matching her.

When we found out about her, she'd just had her six-month health check and there were no longer any concerns about her head size. It had been put down to a family trait.

We were left the PAR to read and I had to ring our social worker the next day to confirm whether we wanted to go ahead or not. She didn't show us a photo as she wanted us to be sure we wanted to proceed based on the information in the report and not be swayed by a picture.

There were still concerns about her development, but without a crystal ball, you can never know how a child is going to develop. That night we read the report over and over, not really believing how lucky we were. We really couldn't have hoped for a child any younger.

The more I read the report, the more I knew she was our daughter. That's how I hoped it would be. That we both felt the same and wanted to proceed. Some people get an instant connection, some have more of a feeling that there's no reason to say no. I think you'll know if it doesn't feel right.

If you've got a partner, you obviously both need to be in agreement about proceeding. If one of you isn't, don't be afraid to ask your social worker to come out again and talk things through.

When I phoned our social worker the next day to say we wanted to go ahead, I thought she was going to say there'd been a mistake. There hadn't and as soon as I said we wanted to go ahead, she sounded so excited for us. She said she hadn't shown us a photograph because she wanted us to be sure we were happy with the level of uncertainty before we fell in love with the photo.

I went in to see her that morning and she gave me the photo in an envelope. It took me quite a while to bring myself to open it. In the end she had to prompt me to do it. I think part of it was I still wasn't letting myself believe that I was going to be a mum.

I'd waiting for so long and had built up a wall to keep my emotions in check. I was too scared to take it down in case I was disappointed again. It was a weird feeling seeing the photo. I'd wanted to save it for when I was with my husband but he'd told me to look at it. It was a beautiful photo of a little girl with the biggest blue eyes I'd ever seen. I still didn't let myself feel anything for her though. I was too scared it would all go wrong.

It was the 31st July when we found out about our daughter, right in the middle of school holidays. Our social worker wanted to try and get everything done for the August Panel as she was out of the country for the September Panel.

Unfortunately, although we met our daughter's social worker and foster carer quite quickly, the medical adviser was away until the end of August, after the Panel date so a quick Panel date didn't happen.

I was very nervous when we met her social worker. I was convinced that once she met us, she'd change her mind. I still couldn't quite believe that our dreams of becoming parents were going to come true. I was expecting that we'd be grilled about everything from how we intended to parent to how long I'd be taking for adoption leave.

In the end, the meeting was quite short. We had a few questions about birth mum, siblings and contact but I don't remember her asking us very much at all. She had a quick look around the house and that was about it. I don't know what I really expected, but it felt very brief and detached.

The types of questions you need to ask your child's social worker will vary depending on their circumstances. If there are known issues, ask what support is in place and whether that will continue. If not why not? If it will, how will it work exactly?

I felt we got much more out of the meeting with her foster carer. I had a list of questions about practical things like what size nappy she was wearing and what foods she liked, but it didn't really occur to me to ask what our little girl was like!

It's such a weird situation to be in. You're meeting the person who has cared for the little person someone else has picked to be your child.

Even though we knew everything was approved by everyone who needed to, other than Panel, I was still expecting something to go wrong. I really struggled to let myself believe it was going to happen so still felt very detached and was therefore only focusing on the practical side of things.

It was actually our social worker who asked the foster carer what our little girl was like. Looking back, she must have thought we'd lost the plot. We were about to become parents to a little girl we'd never met, and all I wanted to know was nappy size and how she slept!

It's a good idea to ask the foster carer at that first meeting, what things your child will be coming home with. Then you're not wasting money buying stuff they already have, or not having something vital that you thought they would have. We were told our daughter would be coming home with her current sized clothes, toys, dummies and bottles. She would also have some keepsake items such as the clothes and blanket she came out of hospital in.

The meeting with the medical adviser was informative and gave us a bit more insight into some of the issues. It was lovely to hear about how much progress she'd made and that, although no-one knew how she was going to develop, there were no medical concerns about her. The doctor is an adoptive mum and it gave me goose bumps hearing her talk about her daughter and how excited she was for us.

The types of questions you ask the professionals will depend on what the issues are with your child, their age and circumstances. The point of the meetings are to share information so that you're armed with as much insight as possible to make the transition from foster care to your home as easy as possible. It will also prepare you for what you may have to face in the future. Make a list and read from it if you need to.

Name

Obviously, by the time you get to know about your child, they will have a first name. Their surname will change to yours once the adoption order is granted, but changing their first name needs to be something you think about very carefully before you do it. It's a huge thing to change it because it's part of their birth identity.

The age of your child will be a big factor. The younger they are, the less likely they are to recognise their name. Security may be an issue if your child has a particularly unique or distinctive first name. You may be advised to change it to something that doesn't stand out so much.

The important thing to remember about a first name is that it's the name your child's birth family picked for them. It's part of who they are and their birth history. It may not be what you would've picked, but it's their name.

Changing it completely can be seen as trying to wipe out that connection with their birth family. I've read several blogs from adult adoptees who were angry that their birth name had been changed completely by their adoptive parents.

If you really don't like the first name, there's a risk it could affect how you bond with your child so it isn't a straight forward issue. If you're considering changing your child's name, speak to your social worker about it.

Both our children were young babies when they came home. They have unusual birth first names which we were concerned could cause problems. Eldest knows her birth family picked her second middle name. She doesn't like it at the moment because it's usually a boy's name.

We've changed their birth first names, but kept them as middle names. That way, when they're older, if they want to be known by that name, they can. My mum is known by her middle name as she doesn't like her first name.

Our eldest has a name we picked as her first name, my middle name as her first middle name and her birth first name as her second middle name. She picked our youngest's first name, we picked her first middle name and her birth name is her second middle name. I think that's a nice compromise because there's significance to all of their names.

Both social workers were happy for us to change the names, as long as the birth name was still part of their names. Keeping it as a middle name is a good compromise and keeps a strong link to their birth history.

If your child is talking by the time you meet them, the chances are they will already be attached to their name. It will be difficult to change it in those circumstances, but you could add middle names that you've picked.

There's no hard and fast rule, it will depend on each child and family's circumstances.

Matching Panel

A match has to be approved by the agency's Adoption Panel. If you've been matched with the same agency who approved you, it'll be the same Panel. If you've been matched with a different agency, it'll be the Panel for that agency.

The procedure is pretty much the same as for approval. Your social worker will have submitted a report ahead of the Panel date which will detail why everyone believes the match should be approved. It will contain details of the child, their particular needs and why you are best able to meet them. There'll also be details of any support plan that will need to be in place once the child is home.

Preparing for Matching Panel was a weird feeling. If felt like there was much more at stake than at Approval Panel. It was hard preparing her room and buying clothes, nappies, feeding things, knowing that in theory, that same Panel who decided we could become parents, could say no to our match. I tried not to dwell on that too much, but it was always at the back of my mind.

I think that's what stopped me letting go and getting too excited. I also think that played a part in why it took me so long to fall in love with our little girl. I'd spent so long holding back and keeping my emotions in check, it took me a long time to let that go.

It's also difficult planning with work when you're going to leave because until Panel say yes, everything could still fall through. That kind of thing doesn't just happen out of the blue so you'll be aware if there are issues. It's just another layer of uncertainty to get through.

Our eldest was just under nine months old at Matching Panel. My mum had bought her a lovely teddy bear so we slept with that and a snuggle blanket for a couple of weeks before Panel so that they had our smell on them. We took photos of ourselves and printed them off A4 size and laminated them so that the foster carer could stick them up around their house.

We wanted to make her a photo book of us and our immediate family so that she recognised our faces. My mum printed off the photos onto fabric and made them up into a little book which was safe and durable enough for her to use herself.

The things you give to the foster carers to help prepare your child to meet you will vary depending on your child's age and circumstances. Some photographs, an age appropriate toy or small gift and perhaps something with your smell on are ideal. The photos will mean you're a familiar face on the first day.

I don't think I've ever been as nervous for anything as I was for Matching Panel. It was a Wednesday. I was due to finish work the next day and then intros were to start the following Thursday if we got a yes.

I'm a civil servant so we have a very clear adoption policy which takes into account the fact that Matching Panel happens very close to a proposed start of adoption leave. I can imagine that if you work for a small business, it is very difficult to work all of that out.

Our agency's Panel normally met every third Wednesday of the month but a special Panel had been convened for us the first Wednesday of the month because of the problems we'd had with various people being on leave. Waiting two weeks may not have been that long in the grand scheme of things, but for a nine-month old baby, it's a long time.

The meeting was in the morning and we turned up armed with our laminated photos, the things we'd been sleeping with and the photo book. I was utterly terrified. Writing about it now fills me with overwhelming emotions.

How Panel takes place will depend on your agency and the restrictions in place due to Covid-19. Most are now being done virtually so the format will be the same as described earlier on for Approval Panel.

The format of our meeting was the same as Approval Panel – our social worker and our daughter's social worker went in first and then we were invited in. Straight away the chairman said Panel were going to approve the match. It felt like we were in some kind of parallel universe after that. We still had to sit there and answer questions when all I wanted to do was cry.

I don't really remember much about the questions but I think they were to do with why we thought this was the right match and how much time I was taking off work. Knowing why you think you're right for the child can be a difficult one to answer. My advice is be honest and answer from your heart. An emotional connection with a child is a good starting point to build on.

As with Approval Panel, the decision has to be approved by the agency's decision maker. I can't think of a reason why it wouldn't be, but it's another box that has to be ticked. This takes 10-14 days. Introductions don't usually start until this is done (although they did for our youngest).

You'll get a matching certificate from your social worker which you'll need to copy and give to your employer so that your adoption leave and pay can start. We got the certificate on panel day.

Planning meeting

Straight after the Panel, we had a planning meeting with our social worker to sort out the detail of introductions (or transitions). Again, when and how this happens will depend on your agency, but it should be around the time of panel. Some do it before, some after. This should give you all the detail you need to know about timings, where you need to be, how long each session will last, who is doing what and the length of introductions.

If introductions are happening when Covid-19 restrictions are in place, they may start off virtually, so you'll need to know how long this part is and when physical introductions start. There may also be a requirement for you to isolate first so all that information should be in the plan.

We were given an A4 sheet of paper showing the detail of each day. If there's anything you're not sure about don't be afraid to ask. If you're anything like me, you need to know about food and meals. We knew from the plan when we'd need packed lunches for us and when we'd need to provide food for our daughter. Make sure you keep a copy of this as it's a great tool to use for life story work later on.

Our introductions were originally going to be only six days long which seemed to me to be such a short period of time to get to know our little girl. However, there was planned industrial action on the day she was originally supposed to come home so introductions were extended by one day. We were going to meet her the Thursday and then if all went to plan, bring her home for keeps the following Wednesday.

Going into work the day after Panel knowing it was going to be my last day there for just over a year was weird. I was excited but also terrified. The longest I'd ever been off work was three weeks and I didn't know if I would cope being away that long.

There were a lot of changes going on and I was worried I wouldn't be able to do my job by the time I went back. I was in tears driving home because I couldn't believe that after all the years we'd been trying to become parents, it was finally going to happen.

I'm glad I had a few days to myself before introductions started and would definitely recommend doing that if you can. I had a pamper day with my sister and did last minute shopping and lots of cooking so that we had a stocked freezer for us and also for our daughter.

She was struggling eating foods with lumps in so after doing lots of reading, I decided to go back a stage and give her lots of pureed meals. I spent hours chopping and cooking and then blending all kinds of dishes and putting them into ice cube trays to freeze. I loved doing it as it helped me feel like a mum.

Part 4
Placement and beyond

Introductions

Unless you're fostering to adopt straight from baby being born, there will have to be a period of introduction to your child. This is sometimes called transition.

Basically it's as the name suggests, an introduction to your child at the foster carers and then your home. They last from five or six days up to a couple of weeks depending on the age of the child. If it's siblings, they may last longer.

The detail of the introductions should be given to you after matching Panel. There should then be a meeting just before introductions start to make sure everyone knows what is expected to happen.

Your child needs to get to know you and vice versa. It would be extremely upsetting for them if a complete stranger turns up and takes them away without them getting to know you a bit first.

They need to meet you in the foster carer's home so that they can learn to start transferring their attachment to you in an environment which is safe for them. As introductions progress, you will take over the care of your child, taking them out and to your home.

There should be regular reviews with social workers to check how things are going. The timescales can be reduced or extended if needs be. There will be a final review meeting on the last day to make sure everyone (including you) agrees that the child should be moved to your home.

Be prepared that introductions are emotionally draining. You're getting to know your child (or children) in front of people who've been caring for them for a long period of time. You're in a strange environment and it can feel like you're under the spotlight.

The night before introductions started with our eldest was surreal. I was excited but utterly terrified; terrified our daughter wouldn't like me but also that I wouldn't like her.

Meeting our child was the part of the process that worried me the most. What if it just felt wrong? Or even worse, what if it felt right for my husband but wrong for me or vice versa?

Unsurprisingly, I didn't sleep much the night before we met her. My mind was going over and over things and I was trying to second guess how I would react and what she would be like. I was also very, very nervous that we wouldn't know what to do. What if we dropped her or put her nappy on upside down?

We were expected to get to know our little girl in a stranger's house. It felt like we were going to be in a goldfish bowl with everyone watching us while we messed up.

Our introduction schedule was detailed so we knew exactly what was expected of us and when. That really helped us plan and decide where to go, what food we needed and things like that. As long as I know whether I need to take my own food and where the toilets are, I can cope with most things a lot better.

For the first day, it will really help if you're wearing the same clothes you had on in the photos you've given to the foster carers to show to your child. That helps with recognition straight away. Also, if you've given them a snuggle toy which has your smell on it, wear the same perfume / deodorant / body spray. With younger babies, bright coloured clothes are good, and taking a bag for them to come and explore with toys and safe things for them to play with is a great way of starting to build attachment. It encourages them to come across to you and explore and you can help them to find out what's inside.

I can't remember the exact timings of introduction day, but I think the final planning meeting was after lunch at the council offices. The foster carer was there with our social worker, our daughter's social worker and a social work manager.

We went over the introduction plan again and agreed which social worker would be keeping in touch with us to check everything was ok. I was very glad it was going to be our social worker ringing us, probably every other evening, to check there were no issues. We knew we could ring her whenever we needed to, but I was glad she would be in touch regularly. It's an obvious point, but make sure you've got everyone's phone number, and the full address of the foster carer.

At the end of the meeting, the foster carer left first to get to her house before us so she was ready and waiting for us with our daughter. We then left and our daughter's social worker said she'd meet us at the foster carer's house in about half an hour.

I felt physically sick when we pulled up outside the foster carer's house. This was the point of no return and I was terrified. My husband was quite relaxed and calm and I remember feeling very jealous of him for being like that.

We opened the back gate to be greeted by the biggest pair of eyes I have ever seen. They were full of mischief. My stomach fell through the ground and for the next hour or so, I felt like I was having an out of body experience. It just didn't feel real. We'd waited for so long to become parents so I just didn't believe that it was really happening. I still expected something to go wrong.

My husband was smitten the second he clapped eyes on our daughter. I didn't feel like that. I just felt numb. I felt an instant bond with her, but it wasn't love.

It felt weird going into the foster carer's home, not least because there were photos of us plastered all over the place. Our daughter seemed at ease with us straight away and I think the photos had a lot to do with that. The foster carers had done a brilliant job of preparing her to meet us, even though Panel had only been a week before.

The first session lasted a couple of hours. Our daughter's social worker came to check everything was ok and the rest of the time we just played with our baby on the floor. We asked the foster carer lots of questions about her routine but it all felt very surreal.

Part of me just wanted to scoop her up and take her home, the other part of me was terrified at that prospect. I felt like a fraud and that we wouldn't know how to look after her. I couldn't imagine ever being able to look after her.

The hardest thing about introductions is the fact that they take place in a stranger's home. You have to care for a child you've never met before in front of the people who've looked after the child for often many months.

They know how to care for them. You don't. It's important to remember, it's their job. Part of that job is to make the transition from their care into yours as easy as possible for the child. As with every profession, there's a wide range of quality in foster carers.

It's a stressful time for everyone. The best advice I can give is to be yourselves throughout introductions. Don't be afraid to ask for help and advice. Everyone has different ways of doing things and as a new parent, you'll have ideas about how you want to do things. However, introductions are not the time to try out your new ideas. Be respectful and mindful of the fact that the foster carer will have a lot more parenting experience than you.

That doesn't mean how they do things is better than how you want to do things. But they do know your child and the status quo in terms of routines, food etc is the best way to go until you've brought your child home.

Clearly if they're suggesting things that are simply not safe, you don't do it and take advice in those situations from your social worker. But drinking juice when you'd rather they had water, or sleeping in your arms rather than a cot for nap time, are all things that can be gradually changed once your child is home.

Our foster carer gave us an A4 sheet of paper with our daughter's full routine on it. I treated that like gospel and followed things to the letter because that's what the foster carer did. I was terrified of what would happen if I changed things, even if I didn't agree with them.

Over time, we obviously did make changes, adapting slowly to what would work for our family. The world didn't end and for some things, they were definitely changes for the better. Trust your instincts and go with what feels right for your child. Just not on the first day of introductions.

Our foster carers were brilliant. We were made to feel at home straight away. My husband has the ability to talk to anyone about anything and it doesn't feel strained. I can't and often struggle with small talk so I was very grateful that he was able to do a lot of the talking to start off with. It made me feel at ease and helped me feel able to join in when I was ready.

Day two of introductions was a longer period of time at the foster carer's home. As I've said, our daughter took to us very quickly so on the second day, we were able to do quite a lot of her care.

Unfortunately, she had a virus which produced some pretty hideous nappies. I'll never forgot how panicked I was at having to change those in front of the foster carer. I knew it was something hubby would only do once he felt more confident (he'd never changed a nappy before, I had) so it had to be me. He helped as much as he could, bless him, but it was more arms-length moral support than anything practical!

The foster carer was brilliant. It was clear I was struggling not to get poo everywhere and she offered advice in a way that didn't make me feel stupid. It was a revelation to me to learn that baby vests are designed to be pulled off downwards as well as over the head for these poo fest situations. Genius!

The foster carer was confident enough in our abilities to let us take our daughter out for a walk in the pram. That's a feeling I will never forget. I felt so proud of us, pushing round our little girl. She was fast asleep and perfectly happy in our care.

The foster family lived just round the corner from my mother-in-law so she got a sneak peep of a sleeping baby as we went past. Her face was so full of pride when she saw us.

Day three was our biggest test and probably the day I was dreading as well as being excited for. We had to take our daughter out for several hours including over lunch, but we weren't allowed to take her to our home.

Luckily, the weather was kind to us so we were able to stick to our plan of taking her to our local park. It is huge with a lake and lovely café. I've spent many hours there walking off my worries and soaking in the beautiful surroundings. It therefore felt like the perfect place for our first family outing.

90% of the day was utterly perfect. Our daughter was brilliant and showed no signs of distress at being with us. We walked round the park for hours, literally glowing with pride. We had a snack in the café and my heart melted as our daughter tried to feed her daddy some of her biscuit.

Everything was going well until it became clear the virus had been at work and she had done an explosive poo. One of the reasons we'd picked the park was because the toilets in the café are nice and I knew they had a changing area in the ladies. There was no way hubby was confident enough to do it on his own so I knew it was going to have to be me as unfortunately there wasn't a changing area we could both go to.

I've endured some stressful situations in my life, but I can honestly say changing her nappy that day was one of the worst of my life. I can laugh about it now, but at the time I felt so out of my depth and utterly useless.

For a start, the set up in the changing area wasn't ideal. The changing tray was right beside the door and no-where near the bin or the wash basins. I stripped her off but had made the rooky mistake of not having everything at my finger-tips like an open nappy bag and the wet wipes open and a few already out of the packet.

That was the first time our daughter showed any sign of distress in our care and she very quickly became utterly hysterical. There were a lot of people going in and out of the toilets, and although it was very clear I needed an extra pair of hands, not one person offered any help.

Even a word of encouragement would have gone a long way. One woman very helpfully told me that my "son" had a good set of lungs and laughed as she walked out of the door. By this point I was fighting back the tears and literally up to my elbows in poo.

Somehow, I kept it together and gradually won the battle against the poo and got us both cleaned up. It felt like we'd been in the toilets for hours and by the time we came out, hubby was pacing up and down outside and looked very worried. Not worried enough to try and find out if we were ok by asking someone to come and check on us, but he was very definitely concerned!

I must have looked like I'd done a five mile run as the sweat was dripping off me and I knew my face was scarlet. It's true that you learn from your mistakes and I certainly took all the lessons I needed from that experience. And I know that had it not been for the foster carer's tip about the vest being able to be pulled down not over the head, it would have been a lot, lot worse.

It was only a small blip in what was a beautiful day. I was very proud of us for getting through it together and being able to take care of our daughter in a situation that was way out of our comfort zone.

After the escapade in the park, we had a few hours off to go and buy a new car seat as the one we had was too small for her (we had to borrow the foster carer's for the trip to the park), and then it was back to the foster carer's house to give her tea and do her bedtime routine.

Days four, five and six were an introduction to our home. The foster carer brought her round in the morning of day four, stayed while we showed her round her new room and the house, and then left us with our daughter for the rest of the day.

It was such an amazing feeling when she left. There we were, with our little girl sitting playing happily on the floor with us wrapped round her little finger. She fell asleep on hubby and the look of pride on his face when she did was priceless. We had her all day, then took her back to the foster carer's to give her tea and do her bedtime routine.

On day five, we got a text from the foster carer early in the morning to say our daughter wasn't well so she'd made an appointment at the doctors and for us to meet her there. I'd been ill through the night too so was feeling decidedly wobbly.

The doctor's appointment was awful as it felt like we were doubly under the microscope. Our daughter didn't like us to cuddle her in when she was upset and it was awful trying to soothe and comfort her while the doctor examined her. I could tell the foster carer was desperate to scoop her up and comfort her, but our daughter needed to know that was our job now.

Once that trauma was over, we had her to ourselves for the rest of the day and took her back to the foster carer's for her bedtime routine. By this point I really wanted her to be home. She was starting to get distressed at being taken back to the foster carer which was a good sign that she was starting to transfer her attachment to us.

I can't imagine how hard it must be for foster carers watching a child they've brought up for months, sometimes years, gradually distancing themselves from them and viewing someone else as their primary care giver. I take my hat off to them as I know I couldn't do it.

Day six was the last day of introductions. It was spent at our house again and we took our daughter back home earlier so that the foster family could say goodbye. It also meant we had the chance to relax for our last night as a twosome before our lives changed forever.

Day seven was move in day. I was excited but really nervous about it. Introductions had gone really well, but I was still expecting someone to say "there's been a mistake, this isn't your child".

We had a final review meeting late morning and everyone agreed there were no issues, that introductions had gone really well and that the move home could go ahead (thank goodness).

Again, the foster carer left the meeting first as did our daughter's social worker, then we left and made our way to collect our little girl and bring her home for keeps. The memories of doing that and how I felt are so fresh in my mind. It makes me extremely emotional every time I think about it.

The foster carer had said she needed the pick up to be quick otherwise she would have time to get really upset and she didn't want to do that in front of our little girl. So, we'd prepared ourselves for a swift handover.

We went with thank you cards and gifts for the family and were ready to scoop our baby up and take her home. Unfortunately, despite us giving the social worker a head start, she still hadn't arrived by the time we were ready to go. She had to be there to oversee the hand over and make sure our daughter was given to us rather than random strangers.

It was nearly half an hour before she arrived. By this time our daughter was starting to get hungry and agitated so we'd put her in the car. Again, my husband's ability to talk about anything and everything came into its own. He was able to keep the conversation going until the social worker finally arrived, completely oblivious to the fact that she'd taken so long to get there.

As the car was all packed and ready, we said our final goodbyes and left pretty quickly. I felt so sad for the foster carer. The start of an amazing journey for us was the end of one for them.

I can't really remember what we did for the rest of the day as it all felt surreal. I couldn't believe that after so many years of trying to have a family, our dreams had finally come true. Our little girl was home.

I'll never forget bathing her that night and her being so happy and relaxed with us. I expected the first bedtime to be horrendous but she was utterly amazing. I gave her a bottle, put her in her cot and she went to sleep more or less straight away. That completely blew my mind. We'd taken her away from everything she'd ever known but she wasn't fazed by it at all.

The foster carer asked if I would text that night to let her know she'd gone to sleep which I did. Then hubby and I sat and stared at the baby monitor for most of the evening, straining to check she was breathing, as well as me checking on her pretty much every 15 minutes.

She woke up once through the night for a bottle, but other than that, she slept right through. It still amazes me that she did and has continued to sleep through, other than on a handful of occasions, ever since.

I don't know how we got to be so lucky to have a baby that sleeps so well. It didn't help us to sleep much for those first few nights as even with the monitor on all night (even though she was in the next room and the door was wide open) I must have checked on her every hour. I couldn't believe she had settled so well. We had braced ourselves for having a very distressed little baby, but she took it all in her stride.

Adoption leave and pay

If you've got a partner and you both work, you'll need to decide who is going to be going to work and who is going to be taking adoption leave. Everyone's circumstances are different. Some people can afford to take the maximum leave, some simply can't. Some can afford to but find they need to be back at work, perhaps because being at home all day doesn't work for them. Do whatever works for you.

Your agency will want one of you to be off as long as possible with your child after they're placed. Adoption leave is up to 12 months. How much of that time is paid depends on where you work.

Statutory adoption pay is 90% of your gross average weekly earnings for the first six weeks. After that it is 90% or the statutory rate which is around £145 per week, whichever is the lower amount. Some employers will have the same pay policies for adoption as maternity, some won't so what you get will depend on where you work.

I'm very lucky as I got six months full pay, 12 weeks statutory pay and then 12 weeks unpaid. I'd saved up for a long time to be off with our child so I was able to take the full 12 months.

Apart from the fact that I wanted to be the one taking the leave, it didn't make any financial sense for my husband to be off as he is self-employed. This had a lot of positives in the early days because it meant he could take days off whenever he needed to. Obviously, the downside is he didn't get paid for those days as there is no entitlement for paternity or adoption pay if you're self-employed.

If you are adopting on your own and you're self-employed, you'll need to factor in how you'll be able to afford to take time off.

Once your child is home, you can apply for child benefit. Your social worker should have given you the form to do this, if they don't, ask for it or you can apply online. It takes a little while to process but it will be back dated from the date your child came home.

Meeting family

Our social worker hadn't really talked to us about what happened after placement. After so much planning about who did what and when for introductions, it felt very daunting just being left to it. It also felt quite liberating.

To start off with we had weekly visits from our social worker (our daughter's social worker left the authority not long after she was placed with us so we didn't see her much). There were also reviews and visits from the health visitor. Your child is still classed as being looked after by the local authority until the adoption order is granted. This means the health visitor has to do more visits than for a child that isn't looked after.

I'd read quite a few posts on the adoption forum on www.fertilityfriends.co.uk about how long to leave it before you introduce your little one(s) to family and friends. A lot of people had been told to keep it to just them for quite a long period of time, and then gradually introduce people for short periods of time, but to not let others cuddle or pick up their child. This is "funnelling" and if you google "funnelling adoption attachment", you'll find a wealth of information about the technique.

I'm no expert on the topic so won't try and explain it in any detail, but essentially it relates to building attachments with your child. Parents being the sole care givers (i.e. others not changing nappies, cuddling, feeding etc) can be a good technique to use for adoptive children, and the best way of building a strong attachment. I did ask our social worker about it and whether she recommended that we did it. She was pragmatic as ever and said it was up to us and that she had no strong views about it.

I'd talked to hubby about it and we decided that we should try it, although we were worried how we were going to be able to keep family away for any period of time after our daughter came home! They were almost as excited about meeting her as we were, my two nieces in particular.

I mentioned it to the foster carer at some point during introductions and I'm so glad I did. She was very clear in her advice to us that she didn't think it was the right thing to do for our daughter. She was used to being in a busy household and loved playing with others. She thought she'd struggle with it being just the three of us for a long period of time without meeting others, particularly children.

So, once our daughter was home, we revised our plans slightly about keeping family at arm's length. We did Facetime with both sets of families for the first couple of weeks and then did arranged visits to our house for each set separately so that she wasn't too overwhelmed by lots of new faces.

That seemed to work really well. We'd asked everyone not to pick her up and everyone was quite happy to get down on the floor with her or for us to have her on our knee sitting beside them.

My advice would therefore be to ask the foster carers what they think is the best way of introducing new people to your child. They may not be experts in attachment theories, but they are experts in your child. I'm not saying that their advice should be followed to the letter, but it will give you a feel for what is going to work best for your child. For our daughter, it was definitely better to introduce people early on.

Routines

Being a new parent via adoption is completely different from being a birth parent. When you give birth, your child obviously doesn't have routines or habits, likes or dislikes. They're a tiny new baby that will rely on you for absolutely everything. You learn with your child what they like and dislike, what works for them (and you) and what doesn't.

Having an adopted child is a whole different kettle of fish. They are likely to come with settled routines, will have an idea of what they like and don't like and how they like their day to be structured.

If you're lucky, the foster carer will give you as much of that information as they can during introductions. You'll be able to pick up what is working and what doesn't and any major likes or dislikes. Not only are you trying to get to know your child, you're also trying to learn their routine.

In the early days, I think sticking to what they already do has to be the way to go. You have changed 100% of their surroundings. Changing their routine the day you bring them home in my view, isn't the best thing for your child. In time things can be changed, but not straight away.

Our foster carer had prepared a sheet of A4 paper with our daughter's daily routine on it. That became like the holy grail to me. I panicked if something happened out of sync or we weren't home at the right time for food / nap.

I look back at that time now and wish I could have told myself to chill out a bit more! It was great to have her routine to hand and in a lot of detail, but I felt because it was there, that I had to stick to it.

When it was clear some things needed to be changed, I felt guilty that I wasn't following things to the letter which was a ridiculous waste of energy. If you're lucky enough to get a detailed routine from the foster carer, follow it as much as you can to start off with, but don't be afraid to change what doesn't work. It's a fantastic guide, but once your child is home, you're the one parenting them.

I was a lot more relaxed with our youngest. We had the same detailed routine written down, but I changed some things quite quickly like nap times. We started weaning the day after she came home so some things had to change. Plus, with our youngest, our eldest had recently started school so her routine had to be tweaked to fit around school runs.

If you don't get a detailed routine, it's going to be a question of trial and error to work out when the best times are for food / naps / play etc, depending on the age of your child. That can be really hard. There's a wealth of information and advice on the internet about sleep routines so that's a good place to start.

Naps were a big thing for me. Both children tended to nap either on someone or in their pram or bouncy chair at the foster carer's. As much as I loved them both snuggling in for a sleep, they didn't sleep very well like that or for very long. During introductions I tried our eldest in her cot for a nap and was pleasantly surprised when she took to that straight away and had a decent nap in it.

That was the only big change we made to her routine early on. Wherever possible, her naps were in her cot, certainly for her main afternoon one. For the first week or so, I was more than happy for her morning short nap to be snuggled in to me, but the more she got used to her cot, the more she preferred to nap in there.

Being realistic

Becoming a parent is a rollercoaster, however it happens. Having the responsibility for keeping another human being alive can be overwhelming. If you're going to survive parenthood, you need to be realistic.

Despite the image that can sometimes be portrayed on social media in particular, you don't need to be perfect to keep your child alive and well. Sleep, food and drink, and having essentials like nappies if you've got a baby, are the kinds of things you should focus on for those first few weeks. Anything else is a bonus.

No matter how many books you read, or people you quiz for advice, nothing really prepares you for parenthood. My biggest piece of advice about preparation is food. Make sure you have lots of easy food in your cupboards and freezer.

I did a lot of batch cooking and I'm so glad we had that to fall back on to start off with as it was one less thing to have to worry about. We'd been told that our eldest didn't like lumps in her food so I decided to go back a stage with weaning so made lots of thick purees and froze them. That meant I had a couple of weeks' worth of food ready for her which was brilliant and made things a lot easier.

Don't except things to be perfect. They won't be and for some they won't ever come anywhere close to that. Take things slowly and don't expect too much from your child or yourself.

You need time just being together so that your child can learn who you are and that they can trust you. You've taken them away from all they've known so you can't expect them to love / trust / like you straight away. You need to get to know each other and how things will work best for you together.

The first few weeks and months that our eldest was home passed in a haze for me. There were some amazing moments, a lot of laughs like our first poo in the bath (I screamed, grabbed the baby and left my husband to deal with the poo). The first time she snuggled in, her first word, her first crawl and so many other firsts that we felt very honoured to experience.

I found those first few months very difficult though. The day to day tasks of being a parent were ok once I got into a routine. The part I struggled with was my feelings. I knew she was meant to be my daughter from the moment I read her report. When I first saw her my heart melted and I felt a connection to her. I didn't love her though. That took a long time to develop.

I remember feeling very jealous of my husband because he loved her from the second he clapped eyes on her. I'd read a lot of posts on Fertility Friends about it sometimes taking time for the love to develop. I'm so glad that I did otherwise I think I would have completely freaked out.

I think it was a combination of factors for me. I'd wanted to be a mum for so long and was so over the moon that we'd been matched with a baby girl. I would have been thrilled with whatever child we'd been matched with, but it felt extra special that she was so young. During our long 10 month wait to be matched, I'd built up in my head what it would be like to be a parent and how I'd feel. The reality was never going to live up to the image I'd created.

There was also another dimension to it for me though. My work meant I was only too aware of each part of the process and that until we had the adoption order, she could be taken away from us.

I'll explain the legal process in more detail later on, but basically, until an adoption order is granted by the court, they aren't legally your child. You share parental responsibility with the local authority and if birth parents are able to show the court that they are now able to safely parent, the court could say that the child should live with them. That doesn't happen very often and there are a lot of hoops that would need to be jumped through first.

Birth mum didn't engage with the assessment or court process so I knew it was very unlikely she would do anything to oppose the making of the order. Knowing that in theory she could, made me hold back a bit I think from our eldest. I couldn't let myself love her until I knew she was legally our child.

In a way I wanted birth mum to respond to our application. I wanted her to fight for the baby she'd grown in her tummy because I couldn't understand how she'd let her go. I couldn't get my head round the fact that she didn't engage and fight for the right to parent this gorgeous little human she'd grown and nurtured in her body for nine months. I know it wasn't as black and white as that for her, but I wanted her to fight for her little girl.

I'd read about faking it til it comes naturally and that really helped me get through those early months. I knew the love would come so I tried not to dwell on it too much and tried to concentrate on enjoying as much as I could of those early experiences with her.

I didn't talk to anyone about it other than my husband because I trusted that it would happen and it did. Gradually, our precious little girl crept into my heart until I felt the all-consuming love I'd longed to feel for her.

I expected to feel the same way about our youngest and that it would take time for the love to grow. I was very surprised when I fell head over heels with her the second I met her. She looked very much like her big sister did at that age and has big blue eyes just like her so it felt natural that I loved her straight away.

I don't know how it is the first time you hold your child after you've given birth. Holding your adopted child for the first time can feel very surreal. They're a complete stranger to you and you to them. It therefore takes time to get to know them.

They've been moved from a significant carer in their lives so it's going to take them time to get to know you and trust you. Spending one to one time with your child, at their level and at their pace is crucial. You'll hopefully lose hours playing on the floor letting them show you how they like to play.

If your child is a baby, a sling or baby carrier might be a good idea as they're a great way of bonding. I didn't consider this until our eldest had been with us for quite a few months and she wasn't interested in letting me put her in a carrier when I eventually tried it. We went to a sling library for a one to one consultation which is a great way of finding out what type of sling or carrier suits you best. I was really disappointed she didn't take to it.

Swimming is another great way of bonding with your child, particularly if they're a baby. The main problem with swimming with a baby though, is working out how to get them and you changed safely, particularly if they're starting to move.

My first trip to the pool with our eldest was a joint effort with my sister and two nieces. She was about 10 months, wasn't quite crawling, but was wriggling and rolling all over the place. It took the four of us to get her changed and I was ready for a lie down by the time we got into the pool.

The first time I ventured swimming on my own with her, we went to a pool where I could take the pushchair onto the poolside. I thought I had it sorted and got us both into the pool in one piece and with plenty of energy to spare.

The night before, hubby and I had spent a long time blowing up an inflatable ring so that she could float about in it. It was great in the pool and she loved it. The problems came when it was time to leave.

It turns out her adorable swimming costume complete with tutu wasn't quite as practical as it was cute. The tutu meant she was wedged in the inflatable and it took me what felt like a very long time to get her out. I could see the lifeguards trying not to laugh as I tried desperately to get her out of the inflatable without dropping her head first into the pool. Needless to say, that was the one and only time I took the inflatable and it went into the charity bag when we got home.

The early days of our eldest being home are a bit of a blur. We've got lots of photographs but I don't really remember a great deal of it. I do remember having mixed feeling about my husband going back to work. He'd taken about three weeks off work for introductions and her coming home.

I was looking forward to trying to start getting into a routine with her which was far easier if hubby was at work. I was terrified though about how I'd cope. How on earth was I going to be able to keep her safe and alive on my own?

I did keep her alive though and we started to settle into a routine that worked for us. I've said this a lot throughout this book, but we are very lucky. Both children settled very quickly and easily into our care and I didn't really feel there were any issues relating to their history in those early days.

It was the usual parenting dilemmas that kept me on my toes all day. They were both used to quite a good routine with the foster carer and I managed to keep more or less to that for quite a while afterwards, for our eldest in particular.

At nine months our eldest was having a morning nap for about an hour and then a longer afternoon nap. I knew the morning nap would be the first one to go so I decided early on that I'd make the most of that while it lasted. That was my cup of tea, watch trashy TV / read a book or magazine me time.

Having some time to yourself is so important. Being a parent can be overwhelming and it's easy to lose yourself in all of that. Making some time every day just for you is vital. Even if it's only 15 minutes while you have a shower or a bath, make sure you get some just to be you.

Using the morning nap to catch my breath really helped in the early days. I tried to do jobs when she had her longer afternoon nap, but the morning one was my time to relax. I was very sad when they stopped!

Everyone always says that you should sleep when your baby sleeps. That probably works for some people but it didn't for me. There were some times when I was extremely tired and so did sleep during nap times, but I usually woke up feeling worse.

If you're lucky enough to have a child that does have a good nap routine, try and use nap times to do something for you that's relaxing. If napping works for you too, go for it. But if not, read or do your nails or just watch rubbish on TV and give yourself the chance to catch your breath. Parenting isn't a sprint. It's an endurance challenge.

Don't try and cram in lots of housework / cooking / work in the early days. One of the things I learned quite quickly is that you need to prioritise which things around the house are important and which are not. Having a spotlessly clean house doesn't make it a happy, safe and nurturing home.

Post Adoption Depression

This is something that isn't talked about enough. We didn't learn about it during our preparation course or as part of the assessment, I only knew it existed because of posts I'd read on Fertility Friends. I thought that only mums that had given birth suffered from depression as a result of becoming a parent, because it was connected with hormones. It isn't.

Post "becoming a parent" depression affects adopters and birth mum's alike. It's about the overwhelming reality of being a parent. Symptoms include anxiety, overwhelm, panic, guilt, low self-esteem to name just a few. Some also experience physical symptoms like aches and pains, stomach problems and tension headaches.

In some ways, adoptive mums may be more susceptible to it because of everything most of us have been through with infertility, before we've jumped on the adoption rollercoaster. I think we put even more pressure on ourselves to make everything perfect.

I certainly had an unrealistic expectation of what parenthood would be like first time round. I'd built it up in my head for so long and it was never going to live up to what I thought it was going to be like.

Parenting is hard. Parenting an adopted child can be extremely hard. Adopted children often have additional needs due to the life experiences they've had with their birth family, or perhaps due to a life limiting condition. Realising parenthood isn't all love and sparkle is tough.

Don't suffer in silence about how you're feeling – suffering new parent blues is very common. Being tasked with looking after a human being is hard. It is extremely rewarding too but the day to day can be very hard, particularly until you get into a routine that suits everyone.

Talk to you family and friends, your social worker or your health visitor if you have a good relationship with them. It doesn't matter who you talk to, as long as you talk. It may be you will need to talk to your GP if your symptoms are severe.

You're not a failure for feeling overwhelmed so don't suffer in silence if you experience symptoms of post adoption depression. There's some great information on the Mind and Adoption UK websites about depression, the signs to look out for and other advice.

I suffered a lot more with low moods and feeling overwhelmed with our youngest. Not so much because I felt I couldn't cope with two children, but because of the fact that school runs really limited the time we had to get out and about.

My weekdays consisted of getting up, feeding the baby, fighting with the five year old to get her to eat her breakfast / dressed/ clean her teeth / hair done and out of the door in one piece by 8.40. Hubby generally leaves for work before 8am so misses out on the last-minute mayhem of trying to get our eldest ready for school.

It was then a dash to get home before the baby fell asleep for her morning nap. That nap was the only real me time I had. About 40 minutes to myself where I could drink a hot cup of tea and try and pull myself together to face the rest of the day.

Once the peace was shattered it was snack time then we had about an hour and a quarter to get out and do what we needed in terms of shopping or visiting people. It often ended in disaster with the queue being too long which meant we were late getting back for lunch so she was hysterical. Food and bottles ALWAYS take longer to cool when you've got a high-pitched scream piercing your ear drum.

Then it was afternoon nap straight after her lunch. I'd have my lunch, tidy up a bit, do some washing, think about what to have for tea and before I knew it, she was awake and it was a quick snack for her before off again to collect her big sister from school. Then baby's tea when we got back, then our tea with the eldest, then clear up, then bedtime. Repeat. Five days a week.

Not being able to get out and about much really got to me. With our eldest there were no real time constraints. It didn't matter too much if lunch was a bit later because she could sleep later and we still had a couple of hours after she woke up to go out and about if we fancied it.

Both children really thrive on being in a good routine so in the early days, it was worth giving up some out and about time to make sure we stuck to it as much as we could. All children are different. Some thrive on routine, some don't. You'll soon learn what works best for your child.

I found that talking about how I was feeling to my friends and family really helped. As did trying to squeeze in some me time and some exercise.

We bought a second-hand treadmill and I found that if I hadn't been able to get out and walk in the fresh air, walking on there for 20 minutes with my music blasting was a complete tonic. Some people may need more than that so a visit to your GP may be what's necessary. Everyone is different.

The important thing is to know that it's completely normal. No-one is perfect and in parenting you will make mistakes. But that's how we learn and grow as families. So please don't be afraid to ask for help

To tell or not to tell

Which people you tell that your child is adopted is a personal choice. I don't want being adopted to be a big thing for our children. Clearly it is. It's massive that they can't grow up in their birth family, but I don't want it to feel massive to them.

I want them to grow up knowing they grew in our hearts and not in my tummy and to be curious about that and ask whatever questions they want to. It isn't a taboo. It's a fact. I don't want it to define them though. My mum didn't go round introducing me as her birth child so it does feel wrong introducing the fact that my children are adopted into the conversation with people I don't know.

I remember feeling really uneasy with a conversation in one of the baby groups I took our eldest to. As I've said before, I'm not the best at making small talk and conversations about birth and breast feeding are ones I'd managed to avoid like the plague by gently pushing our eldest in another direction so we moved out of the way of the conversation.

One conversation I couldn't slide away from because it was just between myself and another mum, was about how much she said my eldest looked like me. She was talking very animatedly about how it was so unfair that she did all the hard work carrying and growing her children for nine months, and they all look like her husband. She kept saying how much my daughter looked like me.

It was only a few months into placement and I was still feeling very much like a fraud mum. I was expecting someone to say "you're not a proper mum because you don't have a clue what you're doing". Hearing someone say over and over how much my daughter looked like me was lovely, but the whole conversation made me feel like a fraud.

Should I have interrupted her mid flow and said "actually she's adopted so I didn't grow her in my tummy"? I didn't know the lady other than to say hello to in the class. She knew nothing about me or my daughter but I'm pretty sure she wasn't prying. She was just making conversation about how much she thought my daughter looked like me.

The instructor knew that she is adopted but no-one else did. That wasn't because I didn't want to tell anyone, it just wasn't the kind of class where there was much time for chat. We always got there just as the class started because of nap times and travel, so we didn't really have much chance to mix.

Telling people is just something you have to figure out as you go along. The fabric of your family and how it came to be your family is deeply personal, however it happened.

Statutory reviews

Your agency has a duty to make sure your child is being looked after appropriately once they've been placed with you. These checks can be a blessing and a hindrance. It can feel like an extra layer of scrutiny while you're learning how to be a parent and getting to know your child.

With our eldest, I quite liked the fact that our social worker came round a lot. To start off with, it was once a fortnight. They were statutory visits but our social worker quite often stayed for about an hour. Not because she was checking up on us, but because she loved seeing our daughter.

After the first formal review, they got less frequent and were usually about once a month. I was quite sad when they ended following the granting of the order as we got on really well with our social worker and I enjoyed her visits.

The post placement reviews are a formal check to make sure everything is going ok and if they're not, to identify what help and support is needed for you as a family. Those who attend may differ in each area, but for us first time round it was the independent reviewing officer, our social worker and the health visitor. Our eldest's social worker should have been there but she left the authority not long after placement and I don't think she attended any of the reviews.

The first review is within four weeks of placement, the second within three months of the first review and if a third one is needed, within six months of the second review.

The reviews are held at your home (or virtually if restrictions are still in place) and our experience of them is that they are informal. We were very lucky and didn't have any particular issues following the placement of either child, so it may not be as informal for everyone. If there are things that you feel are not being addressed by the local authority, this is a chance for you to air them so they are minuted and a plan agreed as to how the issue can be resolved.

In addition to there being statutory requirements for the number of social work visits in the early months of placement, there are increased visits from your health visitor. For a birth child, health visitors visit regularly during the first six weeks, but then the visits become much less frequent although you can ask them to come out if you have any issues.

With our eldest, the health visitor was the same one she had been seeing ever since she was born. It was decided it would be of benefit for her to have the same health visitor because she knew of the issues in the first few months of our daughter's life. With hindsight, I'm not sure that was the best decision for us. I often felt that things that weren't really an issue, were being seen as an issue because the health visitor knew about the history.

An example of that is the fact that little Miss didn't really like lumps in her food. This was brought up in our initial meeting with her foster carer and the medical adviser. We were told it could be a sign that her mouth and throat muscles weren't developing properly which could lead to speech problems.

It's something that the health visitor made a big thing out of too. I'd talked to my sister and mum about it and they suggested going back a stage with weaning which is what I did. I blended lots of things and gave her that for the first few weeks with finger food.

I gradually made the purees with more lumps in and there were no problems at all. It turns out that her issue was that she didn't like bought pre-made meals. I've since read that babies fed bought baby food are more likely to not like lumps. I've no idea why that is.

Another example of the health visitor jumping to conclusions, I felt, just because our eldest was placed with us for adoption, was to do with her not letting us cuddle her when she was upset. Our eldest settled very well with us and didn't really show any signs of distress. She played happily with us and had no issue being picked up and cuddled.

However, if she was upset as a result of a bump or teething pain, she wouldn't let us cuddle her in. She was happy to be picked up, but she kept her arms wide or kept them as a barrier between her and us.

Our worst experience of this was when she'd been home about six weeks. We'd booked a photo shoot in a local park so that we could give gorgeous photos of our daughter to family as Christmas presents. The photographer propped up our little girl in the base of a tree and started snapping away. We were close by so she could see us and she was quite happy to start off with.

Unfortunately, after a few shots, she very gracefully fell face first out of the tree into a bed of leaves. It was a very short drop and she didn't hurt herself at all, but clearly was very shocked. I scooped her up to check she was ok and try and soothe her. She was hysterical and wouldn't let me cuddle her in at all.

I felt awful. I was convinced a passer-by would come up to me and say that I wasn't a proper mum because I couldn't soothe my baby when she was upset. It felt like the crying lasted for hours. The reality was it was about a minute, she calmed down and happily sat for lots more photos, with us holding on to her tightly.

We mentioned the fact she wouldn't let us cuddle her in to the health visitor, expecting to get some reassurance from her that it was normal. She looked very concerned and said it would need to be closely reviewed because it could be a sign of autism.

I was very shocked by this response. I'd done some reading around autism during our assessment, but had understood diagnosis couldn't be done until about the age of three. No other explanation was suggested by the health visitor for this behaviour and we were left feeling very concerned.

Luckily, we had a visit from our lovely social worker not long after that and told her. She was shocked at what the health visitor had said and reassured us about the most likely reason for the behaviour.

She said she would have been concerned if our daughter let us cuddle her in when she was upset so early on in placement. She was keeping us at arm's length until she properly trusted us and had transferred her attachment from the foster carers to us. If she had let us cuddle her in straight away, it would have suggested she didn't have a strong attachment to the foster carers which would have been more of a concern.

This phase probably only lasted a few months and I will never forget how I felt the first time she let me cuddle her properly. I cried a lot because it was one of the first times I'd really felt like her mum.

Health visitors are a great resource but sometimes it's best to be cautious about what they say. They are great for weight / feeding advice / services in the area, but from my experience, they aren't trained to deal with adopted children and the kinds of issues they are likely to be affected by.

If ours had, when we asked about our daughter not letting us cuddle in, she would have reassured us about the most likely reason for it, rather than causing us unnecessary worry. If you have concerns about behaviour or development, I would speak to your social worker about it first. They'll be able to say whether it's normal behaviour in the context of your child's history, or something that you need to be concerned about. If it's the latter, I think I would ask them who they recommend you seek help from.

Is it because they're adopted?

Being a parent can be very hard and challenging. Your child doesn't arrive with an instruction manual giving detailed answers to every scenario you'll ever encounter. As a new parent, you'll probably feel like you're making it up as you go along.

I felt like every other mum I saw as I was out and about, looked like they knew exactly what they were doing, but I didn't. I was sure someone would come up to me and say "you're not doing it right, give the child back".

Being an adoptive parent can have a whole different dimension of stress added to it. As I've said before, all adopted children have suffered trauma, even if they have never lived with their birth family.

For some children, the issues and conditions that they suffer as a result of their experience will already be known. There may be assessments already done so you can try and prepare for the types of situations you're likely to encounter. This won't be the case with a lot of children and it's a case of learning as you go. This is particularly the case for younger children.

Our social worker drilled into us the fact that because our eldest daughter was a young baby when she was placed with us, there would be a lot of uncertainties about her development. It's hard enough being a first-time parent, without always second guessing whether a particular type of behaviour or issue is normal, or is it because they're adopted?

I found myself doing this a lot early on. Thank goodness for my wonderful sister, mum and friends who had kids and were able to say "it's normal."

I'll never forget talking to my sister about tantrums from our eldest. I was very concerned that they weren't normal because she was utterly awful during them and I was convinced there was something else behind them. My sister managed to contain her chuckles as she told me it was completely normal and recounted umpteen situations of one or other of my nieces doing something similar. I can remember seeing my eldest niece have a meltdown in a shop once, but other than that, they'd always been really well behaved when I was around.

Generally, I think knowledge is a good thing. However, knowing that a certain behaviour could be a sign of something to worry about, doesn't always help and can cause your mind to go into overdrive. My advice would be go with your gut. Ask for advice from your support network before you raise it with any professionals. Don't suffer in silence though because that's how things become unmanageable.

Applying for the order

Once your child has been living with you for 10 weeks, you can apply to the court for the adoption order. Whether you do this straight away or whether you wait will depend on how things are going.

If you don't have the order, your child is still a looked after child which makes referrals for support easier. You therefore need to make sure you have the right support for your family in place before you apply. Examples include:

- If your child has particular needs, how will these be managed in the future?
- Do they need counselling or additional support? If they do, has that been set up?
- Have any finances that were agreed at matching stage been set up? If not, when will they be?
- How long will a current support package last and what happens when it ends?

We didn't require any specific support but had asked for help with nursery fees for our youngest. We hadn't intended to adopt again and had done a lot of work to our house and garden rather than saving to fund a future child.

We asked early on whether funding for her nursery placement would be available until she qualified for two-year old funding. I work three days a week and as much as I'd like to give up work, that isn't an option for us so our youngest, like our eldest, goes to nursery for the three days I'm at work.

Without help from the local authority, we would've had to use debt to pay for the fees so we thought we'd ask. It's always worth asking. At the end of the day, by adopting a child you're saving the local authority a lot of money in terms of foster care, so funding things like nursery should be agreed.

Ours was so once our youngest started nursery, the local authority paid the equivalent of the two-year funding which is 15 hours. We made sure this went into the matching report so we had it in writing. We contacted post-adoption support when it was time for her to start nursery and there were no issues with it being set up.

In terms of applying for the order, some agencies do this for you, others expect you to complete the form with some help from them. Some pay the court fee, others don't so it really will depend on your agency as to how this works.

Our agency completed the form for us and they pay the fee, but they have a convoluted way of doing this. They paid us the fee when we were paid our mileage for introductions, but then we have to give them a cheque to take to the court office with the application form.

We discovered the night before this was to be done that we no longer had a cheque book. So, it ended up with the court ringing me so I could pay the fee over the phone. If you're married, you'll need to submit your marriage certificate which the court then keeps until the order is made. It's worth writing yourself a reminder that the court has the certificate so that you don't spend hours looking for it if you find you need it before the hearing.

The court process is being reformed in line with the digitalisation programme that Her Majesty's Courts and Tribunals Service is currently undergoing. The new system should mean that you can track the progress of your application online which will be a much better way of finding out what's happening.

In a lot of ways, the court part of the process is the bit you have the least control over and unfortunately, often has the most delay. It's also the part of the process that adopters get told the least about which can make it extremely frustrating.

Once your application has been checked and the fee paid, it will be considered by a lawyer to decide which level of judiciary should deal with it. Sometimes it will be Magistrates, sometimes it will be a Judge. Who deals with the application doesn't really matter and usually depends on who concluded the care proceedings so that there is continuity if possible.

When your application is allocated, the court will send out notice of the application to birth parents. The actual application isn't sent to them because it contains the adopter's details. The child's social worker will have spoken to birth parents about the application so they will have an idea as to whether they're likely to agree to it or not.

A lot of birth parents at this stage, will say they won't agree with the application. Saying you will oppose the order and actually doing something about it when the notice arrives are two different things.

Obviously, the circumstances of each birth parent are different. However, a lot come from a background of vulnerability and lack of support. Filling in forms, attending appointments with solicitors and turning up for court appointments is a big commitment.

That's what they have to do if they want to oppose the application once they receive the notice. Saying no to a social worker can be done easily, actually opposing the application requires a lot more.

If the form says birth parents won't agree to the order, it is for the court to decide whether their consent should be dispensed with. So that everyone knows why the local authority are asking the court to do this, they have to file a statement and report detailing why it is appropriate. This will contain a lot of the information which the court has already seen.

Your social worker will also prepare a report about you and how your child has settled. The reality is that in a lot of cases, nothing will have changed in birth parent's circumstances since the care and placement orders were made. This means that even if they do turn up at court, any application they make to ask to oppose the adoption order won't be successful.

Birth parents have to be told that they can attend the hearing and can ask for permission to oppose the making of the order. This can give them false hope that they're going to get the chance to parent their child. More often than not, the reality is that nothing has changed but it means wounds that were perhaps starting to heal, are re-opened. They go through the trauma of effectively losing their child again when they're told they haven't changed their circumstances enough to oppose the order.

Courts do sometimes give birth parents the opportunity to show how they've changed and give them time to file a statement. To be allowed to do this, they have to show that their circumstances have changed since the placement order was made. For the court to consider removing a child, this would have to be a major change in their circumstances.

Timescales for change will have been fully aired during the care proceedings, and if it had been appropriate for the child, the placement order wouldn't have been made. Effectively, they would need to show that the court was wrong in its decision to make the placement order.

And even if it was wrong, the court would still need to be satisfied that it's in the best interests of the child to be removed from their adoptive parents. That's a big ask.

The delay caused by birth parents being allowed to file a statement is a worrying and frustrating time for adopters, but is part of the court process. There's no getting away from the fact that an adoption order is a draconian one because it means a child can't live with their birth family. The court has to be sure there is no other option.

You need to be aware of the process and the possibility of problems with the order being granted, even though the likelihood of this happening is very small. A lot of adopters say they didn't know about the court process and that this could happen which creates more stress for them when the application is delayed to let birth parents file a statement.

When the court is satisfied birth parents have been served with the notice, a hearing date is set. If it's known that birth parents are not going to agree and will attend, a review hearing might be set first to agree dates for filing statements.

A final hearing is listed which is for the birth parents only. It's clearly not appropriate for adopters to attend this with the child.

This can be a stressful time for adopters because you're not involved in any part of this. Birth parents need to attend court, commit to the process and evidence the changes they say they've made before the court will think about a different course of action. The bar is high.

As difficult as it is, you have to trust that the decision makers are experienced in this field. They are required to ensure that parents are given a fair hearing, but their overriding objective is to prioritise the needs of the child.

Once the adoption order is granted, the court can fix a second hearing which the adopters and child attend. This has become known as the celebration hearing. In some ways it's a bit of an anti-climax because when you go you know that the order has already been made.

Unfortunately, having two hearings is the only way the court can logistically manage the risk of birth parents seeing adopters and potentially following them home which would obviously then risk the placement.

For the order to be made, the child and adopters have to be before the court which is why the second hearing takes place. I know that some adopters feel the hearing is a waste of time and some courts ask whether you would like a hearing.

Our area always has a hearing and I'm glad because although it is an anti-climax in a way, it signifies the end of the process which I think is something that should be marked in some way.

The hearing for our youngest really helped our eldest understand that her sister was with us for keeps. She'd been asking about that a lot as she was clearly worried that her sister would go back to the foster carers.

I think it's a nice thing to do for life story work too. You can have a photograph taken in the courtroom which is a lovely way to commemorate the day. It is part of the journey your family has been on and signifies the end, for many, of professional involvement.

We received an adoption certificate and a lovely card which was signed by the Judge wishing us all the best for the future.

After the hearing

How quickly you get the Adoption Order varies from court to court. We got ours both times within about a week. Once you have the order, you can use it to change your child's name at places like the doctors or school.

Changing their name with the GP should trigger a new NHS number being issued so that from that point on, your child's medical records will be in their adopted name. You may also get a new red book from the health visitor with their new number and name. We didn't get one with either of ours and it's not something I pushed for. I think it's a good tool to use for life story work. The book is mainly used when children are babies until all of their immunisations are done. The books contain a wealth of information about their early days of life and it's appropriate that this is in their birth name.

The order should come with a leaflet about what happens next in terms of birth certificates. You must check that all of the details on the order are correct, spelling of names in particular, because the court sends a copy of the order to the General Register Office.

The information contained in the order is then used to make an entry on the Adopted Children Register. This will then generate a new birth certificate. You will receive correspondence from the General Register's Office to say that the entry has been made and that you can order either a short or full certificate, or both.

The short certificate makes no reference to the child being adopted and is headed "Certificate of Birth". The long form is a full copy of the entry in the Adopted Children Register and gives details of the adoption order. This form is what you will need to apply for a passport and there is a fee for it.

With our eldest, we got the short form certificate free with the notice of registration. This has now changed and you have to pay for both which are £11 each currently. We applied using the standard service and it took less than a week for the certificates to arrive.

Keeping in touch with foster carers

How you keep in touch with the foster carers is entirely up to you. It's also your choice whether you do it at all. A lot will depend on how you got on with them during introductions and the age of your child. Some children enjoy meeting their carers regularly. For some it's too confusing.

Like all professions, there are some amazing foster carers and some not so amazing. We were very lucky and ours were amazing. They were very experienced.

We didn't discuss keeping in touch or meeting up, but foster mum asked us to text the night we brought both children home (four years apart) to let her know they had gone to sleep ok. She also asked for a quick update about a month after placement. I was more than happy to do that.

I take my hat off to foster carers. I don't know how they can open their homes and hearts up to so many children, and watch them move on. I decided I wanted to keep in touch via email so I send updates three or four times a year with some photos. Words will never be enough to express our gratitude to the foster carers. Sending photos and an update helps me continue to say thank you.

It was perfect for us that our youngest daughter was placed with the same carers as our eldest. This made introductions easier for us all, but it also meant the carers could see eldest again. And it brought a bit of her life story to life for eldest. She'd seen the photos of her with the carers when she lived with them, so it was lovely for her to see them again. She really came out of her shell with them which was lovely to see.

Some adopters meet up regularly with the foster carers and are encouraged to do this by their social worker. Others don't keep in touch at all. See how you feel and do what you feel is right for you and your family. There's no guidance about it, it's what works for you all. Foster carers will always be a huge part of our children's lives.

Life story work

At some point after your child is placed with you, you'll receive their life story book. You might have received a book from the foster carers about the child's time with them, but this is something different.

The life story book does what it says on the tin. It explains to the child their life story. How they came to be taken into care, why they couldn't live with their birth family, the court process, living with foster carers and then finding their forever family. This is done in an age appropriate way to help your child understand their history.

I was really impressed with our eldest daughter's book. There were a few facts that were incorrect which I changed, but on the whole, we were really pleased with it.

Youngest's is on a whole different level though. It's brilliant. It has a lot more detail and deals with why she couldn't live with her birth family so well. Big issues are dealt with in an age appropriate way and don't lay blame anywhere. It describes how birth parents had massive problems that they couldn't overcome, but that they love their children very much.

Deciding when the best time is to start life story work will vary from family to family and child to child. It will depend on their level of understanding and age when they came home.

Both our children were babies when they came home so have no memories of their birth parents. I was terrified of starting life story work with our eldest. It felt like a lot of pressure to get it right.

I wanted our children to know as early as possible that they're adopted so that it isn't a big thing for them. Clearly, it is a big thing. Not being able to live with your birth family is massive. I don't want it to feel like that for them though. I want it to have always been part of their lives so they ask questions whenever they want to.

I'd started to tell our eldest, probably from about the age of two, that she grew in my heart. When she was three her nursery nurse was pregnant so it was a good opportunity to introduce the concept that she didn't grow in my tummy. We also showed her her life story book about that time.

A few months before that, she'd completely floored me by asking where her sister was. She didn't really understand what a sister was, it was just a word she'd heard used. I thought I was prepared to answer questions like this, but it turns out I wasn't.

For some reason I hadn't expected it and I didn't know how to respond. I took too long in replying and our daughter had lost interest by the time I opened my mouth to speak so I left it. I was annoyed with myself though. I should have been expecting questions like that and had a response ready.

She talked a lot about having a sister for the next few months so it felt like it was the right time to introduce her life story book. I was worried (I do that a lot!) that we'd left it too late after I'd read a post somewhere that we should have started from the day she came home. As I've said, each child (and each parent) is different and will be ready at a different age. You'll know when it's the right time.

I was nervous going through the book with her for the first time. I thought as soon as she knew she had brothers and sisters, she'd want to meet them. I had a knot in my stomach when I turned the page to show her her eldest sister. But she didn't react the way I'd expected her to at all. She just asked her name and then turned the page.

There are several brothers and sisters and she asked all their names but nothing more. She wasn't fazed by seeing the picture of her tummy mummy either. All in all, I think the first time she looked at it, it went really well.

We left the book where she could get it. I think it's important that she can access it whenever she wants to. The book itself isn't precious, it's the content which is important. We have a CD with it on so I can print it off again if needs be. She needs to be able to dip in and out of it as she pleases.

A few days later she got really upset because she said she wanted to grow in my tummy. That really broke my heart and still makes me upset thinking about it because that's one thing I can't change.

I said that she was very special because she has two mummies and that she grew in one's tummy and in one's heart. She disappeared off into her room and came back with a teddy which she said that she wanted to put into my heart. Cue more tears from me!

Over the next few days and weeks, we could almost see the cogs going around in her mind processing everything. She asked more questions and we answered them in an age appropriate way, but they mainly related to not growing in my tummy. I think a lot of that was because her teacher was pregnant and they'd obviously been talking about her baby growing in her tummy.

As our eldest has got older, she goes through phases of wanting to look at her book a lot, and then not looking at it for a while. She knows her brother and sister's names and we say that they live with their families, but she hasn't asked why she can't see them.

She has actually met one of her sisters, but doesn't know it yet. We've been to a few of the family fun days set up by our local authority for adoptive families, and one of her sisters and her adoptive parents have been a couple of times when we were there. Our social worker introduced us to her parents the first time we went, so we've had a chat each time we're there.

Unfortunately, they didn't want their daughter to know at that point that she has a younger sister, so they didn't know they were sisters. At one of the events, they were actually sat beside each other having their faces painted. That would've been the ideal opportunity for them to start to get to know each other and perhaps start some direct contact.

Life story work is so important for adopted children to help them understand their birth history. However difficult it may be for you (and I really struggled with it for a long time), it's in your child's best interests that it's done as early as possible.

Honesty is always the best option, in an age appropriate way. I hope that because we're open and honest with our children, they'll always come to us when they have questions about their birth history, and that they'll tell us when they want to look for their birth family.

I think I'd want to meet my birth family if I were in their shoes so I hope that they do. I also hope that they let us help so that it can be done in as safe a way as possible. I know that in this day and age, a few clicks on Facebook brings up their birth family. I would be really upset if they did this without telling us because that isn't a safe way of doing it.

I think as adopters, our gut reaction at some point will be to forget that your child has another family. It's natural that we do that. We are the ones who are there, day in day out, caring for our children. We are dealing with often extreme behaviours because of the early life experiences our children have had.

The last thing we want to do is talk about the people whose behaviour caused them so much pain. But it's a part of our children's past and ignoring it often makes things worse.

If your child was too young to remember their birth family or has never lived with them, the earlier you introduce life story work, the better. It's then part of who they are as they grow up and isn't a massive shock to them. Finding out your adopted when you're a teenager is, in my opinion, a recipe for disaster.

A massive part of life story work is keeping up with letter box contact. In my professional life, I'd heard the term letter box contact used many, many times.

I'd imagined that in every local authority office, there was a massive big red post box where all the contact letters were posted and then sorted out and sent to the correct people! In reality, it doesn't work quite like that, but we do send our annual letter to the local authority for them to pass it on.

There's no two ways about it, writing a letter to birth family is very hard. I really struggled the first time. I didn't know how to pitch it. I wanted to shout from the tree tops how amazing our daughter is. But I didn't want to sound like I was bragging to birth parents that we were doing a better job than them.

There are plenty of templates on the internet if you need some help, or contact post adoption support if you'd like some guidance. I keep our updates factual. I tell them about likes, dislikes, how she's doing, what films she loves and what hobbies she has and the content will change as they get older.

I tend not to mention where we go for holidays or anything like that because I don't want to it to sound like I'm saying "look at all the places we take her".

One letter from one of her sibling's family was like that. It didn't tell us anything about how she is, how she's doing at school, the kinds of things she likes to do. Just how many holidays she'd been on. The previous letter had been all about how she'd been diagnosed with a condition so it would have been good to know how she's doing with that now.

At least it is a letter for our children to read when they're older. That's what letterbox contact is all about. It's giving your child a way of learning how their sibling(s) are doing and helps them get a sense of what they're like so that if they decide they want to meet later, they know something about them.

Our eldest knows we do them and she's said she'd like to draw a picture to be included with the next one. As the children get older, hopefully they'll want to be involved more and more.

As hard as it can be, letter box contact is vital and should be done. It is usually once a year so it isn't a big commitment. I know some adopters think it's a waste of time as they don't get a reply.

That's frustrating, particularly when it's other adopters that don't reply with sibling contact. It's important though for your child to see that you've done it so they can see what you wrote about them to show their birth family what they're like.

Our contact is once a year in the summer and is sent to birth parents and all siblings. We did a settling in letter for our youngest when she'd been home about 12 weeks.

Some birth parents will reply, some won't. Ours haven't which is a shame. I think part of the problem is that there isn't really the help and support there for birth families to do this.

As I understand it, they're sent a letter every year saying it's time to do a letter, do you want to? A lot of birth parents won't have the ability to write a reply. They probably don't know where to start. I find it hard so I can imagine it is very daunting for a birth parent, particularly if they don't have access to a computer and would therefore have to hand write it.

I'm sure if someone from post adoption support arranged to see them, or there was some kind of drop in or contact letter writing workshops, there'd be more birth parents replying. This does happen in some areas but not all. It doesn't seem to in our area. I appreciate resources are always very tight within local authorities, but I think this would be a very worthwhile use of resources. But that's just my opinion.

So please make sure you keep up annual contact. It means so much to birth family and it will help your child understand their history as they grow up. It can also give you the heads up about possible problems you may encounter if a sibling is experiencing them, or explain some characteristics in your child.

Our youngest has been very late in getting her teeth. She got two at about seven months, but then nothing until she was over a year. We found out in the first update from her brother's adoptive parents that he didn't have any teeth at all until he was over one so it sounds like it's a family trait.

Siblings

If you adopt a single child, one of the things that needs to be on your radar is that another sibling may come along. When we were being assessed, we were very clear that we wanted to be approved for a single child initially, but we were pretty sure we'd want to adopt again when the time felt right.

It's funny how you think you know how you'll react to a situation and then when it happens, you react in completely the opposite way. I was very lucky and was able to take just over 13 months off when our eldest was placed with us. This consisted of my 12 months adoption leave and then some accrued annual leave at the end.

I was going back to work in the November and our daughter had a phased introduction to nursery starting in the October. The week after I went back to work, I got an email from our social worker to say that birth mum had turned up at hospital 35 weeks pregnant. She said that nothing appeared to have changed since our eldest was born so the plan was fostering to adopt and asked if we want to be considered.

Before our eldest was placed, if you'd told me this would have happened, I'd have said I'd have jumped at the chance of being assessed for the sibling. However, my gut reaction was it wasn't the right thing for us to do.

Our daughter was very unsettled as she was struggling with being left at nursery. I was massively struggling being back at work. Everything felt very stressful and unsettled and the thought of us having a new born added into the mix in a few weeks seemed a step too far.

But my heart wanted to say yes. If we said no, we would be denying our daughter the chance to grow up with her sibling. That seemed very unfair and I wasn't sure how we'd be able to explain that to her when she was old enough to understand.

The plan changed from foster to adopt to care and placement which gave us a bit of time to decide, but it still felt wrong. The few weeks we spent deciding what we wanted to do was one of the most difficult times of my life.

I desperately wanted it to be the right thing for us as a family, but I knew it wasn't. I made myself ill worrying about it, but once we made the decision to say no, it felt right and it has always felt right.

Just because on paper it should be the right thing to do, doesn't mean that in reality it will be. It felt like our daughter needed us to herself. We were still getting to know her and understand what she needed from us to feel safe and secure. If we'd said yes we'd have had a just over two year old and a new born and I really didn't think I could cope with that. I know many can, but I didn't think I could.

I was still on edge about the decision until we'd talked it through with our social worker. She was absolutely lovely. I was worried she would try and persuade us to change our minds but she didn't. She didn't make me feel like we were letting our daughter down by saying no, and that was a really big thing for me.

It was the right decision for our family. I will always feel guilty about it because our decision denied our daughter the opportunity of growing up with her sibling, but that wasn't a good enough reason, on its own, for us to say yes.

We asked if direct contact could be considered which we were told it would be. Unfortunately, it was never put forward by the sibling's social worker and so was never raised with his adopters. I had trusted that it was being dealt with and didn't chase it up until it was too late. So direct contact hasn't happened, but we do get an annual update from his birth parents.

You can't prepare yourself for how you'll feel about being asked to be considered for a sibling. If it is something you think you'd want to do in the future, there's no harm in preparing for it financially straight away. If it doesn't happen, you've got some extra money but if it does, you're prepared.

After we'd said no to the sibling, I did say to our social worker that we'd still like to be informed if birth mum was pregnant again. I was convinced that the sibling we'd said no to would be the last. We were very happy as our little family of three, but something made me ask to be contacted if it happened again.

Fast forward just over two years, and I got an email completely out of the blue from our social worker. As soon as I started reading it I knew what it was going to say. Birth mum was pregnant again.

This time everything felt very different. Birth mum had disclosed the pregnancy much earlier on so there was time to think. Our eldest was settled and happy.

Our main concerns were our age (I was mid 40s and my husband was mid 50s) and the thought of going back to sleepless nights filled us both with horror. As we thought we would be staying a family of three, we hadn't been saving and had spent a lot of money on our house and garden in particular. That meant we were in a worse financial situation than we had been with our eldest. Everything was manageable, but we had quite a large loan and no savings.

We took our time to make our decision although this time from the start I knew it was the right thing for us. We knew that our eldest would absolutely love having a younger sibling and that in the grand scheme of things, debt and feeling old weren't good enough reasons to say no.

So, we said yes. Only time will tell how our eldest daughter in particular will feel about our decision to say no to her other sibling. Seeing her and her little sister get to know each other and play together tells me it was the right decision. If we'd said yes to the first sibling, we definitely wouldn't have considered a third. I do think things happen for a reason.

Financial help with childcare

As your child was a looked after child before they were adopted, there are some things you will be able to get financial help with. One of those things is childcare. From the term after your child turns two, you may be entitled to 15 hours free childcare either in a private nursery or registered childminder. This applies if the child is looked after by a local authority which would be the case before the adoption order is granted, or if they've left care under an adoption order.

This is a big help with the cost of childcare if you're adopting a young child. Beware though that not all private nurseries accept this type of funding. When we were looking for a nursery for our eldest, the one we wanted her to go to didn't have any places left for two-year old funding.

I was really disappointed with this as the nursery was within walking distance which would have been ideal. In the end, the nursery we chose was great and more than happy to take two-year old funding.

As with everything, different places do things differently in terms of how you apply. Our nursery applied for the funding, I think because our eldest was already there when she became eligible. Some places will want you to apply yourself.

Have a look at the help with childcare pages on www.gov.uk for the full guidance about who is eligible, and ask at the childcare provider when you make enquiries.

School

Adopted children are given priority for their first choice when it comes to applying for a place at school. I understand the level of priority does vary slightly from authority to authority and the amount of evidence required to prove their status varies.

When I completed our eldest daughter's application for infant school, I was expecting to have to answer a lot of questions about this. When it came to it, all I had to do was tick a box to say that she had been previously looked after by the local authority. I presume the local authority then check her status. Some areas require you to provide a copy of the adoption order so it will depend on where you live as to what you have to do.

Where we live, an adopted child is guaranteed their first choice of school. For some reason, that felt like quite a responsibility placed on us picking the right school because we knew we would get our first choice. However your authority does it, it should mean that your child gets their first choice of school, not just for infants but junior and beyond.

Once your child is in school, as a previously looked after child, the school will be entitled to apply for pupil premium plus. This is designed to help disadvantaged pupils of all abilities to perform better. There is similar funding available if your child goes to nursery from the age of three (Early Years Pupil Premium).

Again, how it is used will depend on the school (or nursery). At our daughter's school, she gets some school trips, milk and after school clubs paid for. Don't be afraid to ask about it and make sure your child is getting what they're entitled to. I was a bit lax with this and didn't follow up the promised letter explaining what we would get. That meant I paid for some trips in reception, but did ask for others to be paid for.

The school (or nursery) will allocate the funding as they see fit. It is designed to promote the educational achievement of looked after pupils. There's a lot of information about how all of this works on www.gov.uk so I would recommend you have a look there before your child starts school.

If your child is already at school when they come home, there may be a lot of other issues that you'll need to consider. I don't have any experience of that scenario so I'm not going to try and guess at the types of issues you need to consider. What I would recommend though, is having a look on Instagram in particular and following some of the adoption accounts on there using #ukadoptioncommunity as a lot have school aged children and will have experienced the types of issues you need to consider.

Post Adoption Support

Any family that has adopted a child can access help and support from post adoption support at the local authority where they live. Don't be afraid to contact them if you need help. They can help with referrals to things like counselling, therapy and contact with birth family.

It isn't a sign of weakness if you need to ask for help. That's what they're there for. Children who need to be adopted have often suffered a lot of trauma. Sometimes that trauma doesn't affect them until they're in a settled and loving family so it may not have been apparent in foster care.

The local authority can apply for funding from the Adoption Support Fund to provide essential therapeutic services if that's what's needed. It's not something that we've needed to access so far so I don't have any direct experience of it, but First4Adoption and Adoption UK are good places to start looking if you want to find out more about exactly what it is and how it can help. Once again, Instagram is also a good place to connect with people who have had experience of contacting post adoption support for help.

Printed in Great Britain
by Amazon